JoyScope

Daily Inspiration to Nourish Your Heart & Soul

Tiffany Kay

BALBOA
PRESS
A DIVISION OF HAY HOUSE

Copyright © 2012 Tiffany Kay Brett

All rights reserved. No part of this book may be used or reproduced by any means, graphic, electronic, or mechanical, including photocopying, recording, taping or by any information storage retrieval system without the written permission of the publisher except in the case of brief quotations embodied in critical articles and reviews.

ISBN: 978-1-4525-5465-5 (sc)
ISBN: 978-1-4525-5466-2 (hc)
ISBN: 978-1-4525-5464-8 (e)

Balboa Press books may be ordered through booksellers or by contacting:

Balboa Press
A Division of Hay House
1663 Liberty Drive
Bloomington, IN 47403
www.balboapress.com
1-(877) 407-4847

Because of the dynamic nature of the Internet, any web addresses or links contained in this book may have changed since publication and may no longer be valid. The views expressed in this work are solely those of the author and do not necessarily reflect the views of the publisher, and the publisher hereby disclaims any responsibility for them.

The author of this book does not dispense medical advice or prescribe the use of any technique as a form of treatment for physical, emotional, or medical problems without the advice of a physician, either directly or indirectly. The intent of the author is only to offer information of a general nature to help you in your quest for emotional and spiritual well-being. In the event you use any of the information in this book for yourself, which is your constitutional right, the author and the publisher assume no responsibility for your actions.

Any people depicted in stock imagery provided by Thinkstock are models, and such images are being used for illustrative purposes only.
Certain stock imagery © Thinkstock.

Printed in the United States of America

Balboa Press rev. date: 7/18/2012

**To all who have inspired my life
Thank you!**

Introduction

The idea for the JoyScope began as a simple inspiration. I overheard a lady sharing with a friend her less than favourable horoscope that day. Somewhat defeatedly, she had already written off the day to bad luck. Whilst I appreciate that there is a fine art to astrology, I couldn't help but think that it was crazy to allow such negative thoughts to pollute the day. What if, instead there was a source of daily inspiration to offer words of wisdom to nourish the heart and soul?

In that moment JoyScope was born. The intention? To provide an alternative to the "horror-scope" which can sometimes be rather gloomy and fear inducing. JoyScope is designed to offer a fresh and uplifting approach to life. Each day, through questions, examples and reframes, you are invited to view the world from a new perspective. I invite you to take a moment, morning or night, to read and reflect on the day's message and to allow the theme to influence your living. Alternatively, you can hold a question in your mind and randomly pick a page to turn to, allowing the message to find you. As you journey through the year, JoyScope will be your companion encouraging and supporting you to live your inspired and joyful life.

1st January
New Beginnings

The New Year always brings with it a sense of hope and optimism. It is a time of heightened awareness of the limitless potential in our lives. And so we boldly stride into the year with a wish list of our greatest desires. It could be that perfect body or health; the dream career; meeting The One or transforming our relationship; a new home or car, or simply to introduce new life-affirming habits. But isn't it interesting that we make this day, and often only this day, the start of all new beginnings? After all, aren't beginnings happening in every moment of every day? If we rely on the clock, we may not notice every new hour, minute and second that occurs, but if we choose to connect to the present moment, we find that we are always cycling through new beginnings, middles and endings. It's the nature of being human. So perhaps you do have resolutions that feel wonderful to pursue. But if not, or they seem to slide as the year progresses, remember that you are the source of all creation in your life, and you can begin that right now.

2nd January
Follow Your Dreams

The message for today is clear: it's time to follow your dreams. As children, we have endless possibilities in an unlimited world—ballet dancer, princess, footballer or space man. So many choices, so little time! But somewhere between there and now we lost sight of our big dreams. Perhaps there is something you have been considering for a while or maybe a desire or ambition long forgotten that would feed your soul and change your life for the better. It may be different to that childhood desire but it will still be there waiting to be discovered. Today is the day to seize the moment. Make a commitment and take an action that will move you closer to your dreams. You can do it!

3rd January
Ebb and Flow

Today the message from the JoyScope is to follow your energy. Like the ebb and flow of the sea, we experience different types of energy in our bodies. There are times when we are *flowing* when it seems natural to be *out* there taking inspired action. And then there are the times of the softer *ebbing* when we are more drawn to retreating to our *inner* world and reflecting and recharging. Both types of energy are essential to a happy and balanced life. The key is to be able to tune into the energy of your body and to know when to ebb and when to flow. Trust your ability to know which energy is right for you today.

4th January
Your Magnificence

The only thing that holds us back in life is the story we tell ourselves about what we can and cannot do. There are no limits to the possibilities when you step outside your comfort zone and dream big. You don't need to know how it will happen to start the process. Just ask yourself *"if you could be, do or have anything, what would it be?"* Creating the vision is the first step. As you begin to tap into the awareness of what you really want, inspiration will flow and guidance will appear in many forms to support the manifestation of your dream. You serve the world best when you are willing to be the magnificent being you were born to be. Be that way today!

5th January
Relationships

Our lives are really a composition of relationships with loved ones, friends, colleagues and even strangers that we fleetingly interact with on a daily basis. Are you the kind of person you would choose to be around? The message from the JoyScope today is to pay close attention to the way you relate to people. You get to choose what you put into the space in between, so choose wisely! Not because it matters what other people think of you but because our relationships on the outside are usually a good indication of how we will treat ourselves. So it follows that the more loving and gentle you are to other people, the more you will nurture that kind of quality relationship with your inner self. Be the loving person you were meant to be and enjoy the ripple effect both inside and out.

6th January
Matching Desires

Having desires is part of feeling alive. What would you like more of in your life? Be it more money, better health, unconditional love or just good fun, it is totally available to you, you just need to be a match for what you want. Today, take time to focus on how you can create the *feelings* of these desires inside of you. How does it feel to be rich, successful, healthy, loving or playful? When we are able to create the feelings on the inside first, we become a match for what we want. It really is that simple. Bask in the knowledge that as you align yourself with your desires, very good things are on their way.

7th January
Resolutions

Here we are, a week into the New Year. How's it going for you? Are you maintaining your New Year Resolutions? The problem with resolutions is that they are flawed from the onset. When you resolve to be different in some way, the energy pushes against how things have been in the past. Whenever you make something wrong, you set up a loop based on the Law of Attraction (like attracts like), which just creates more of the same—so instead of resolving why not try allowing? Allowing lessens the resistance in you and lines you up with what you really want. What will you allow this year? —a healthy, vibrant body or a fulfilling career, or maybe a relationship with your soul mate? You get to choose. Simply allow it to be.

8th January
Reaching for Life

Are you enjoying the journey? When we realise that we can be, have and do anything we want, setting goals and achieving them is part of life. But the enthusiasm and passion for living comes from the process of reaching for what you want, not just its completion. The journey of moving towards your goals is the fun bit! So if we get too hooked on to having achieved the goal, we miss out on all the enjoyment along the way. Be present to the experiences you are having each day. Know that in every set back, the potential for something even more amazing arises. And when it gets good, milk that experience for all it is worth. That is the joy of being alive.

9th January
Release Fear

When we start a new year with renewed enthusiasm and inspiration and begin to consider all of the possibilities in our life, we can accidentally also activate the part of us that doubts or fears our own success. Our greatest regrets often come from those unfulfilled dreams or unaccomplished goals. Yet whatever prevented us from pursuing them is likely to still be lingering in our psyche unless we have taken the time and space to work it through. And a niggly doubt can still be enough to knock us off track. So today create a safe space to ask yourself what fears have been holding you back. They may be hidden or masked by our inner chatterbox that comes up with all of those seemingly logical reasons why it's not practical or sensible to have what we most want. When you notice any concerns, gently challenge by asking, *"Is that really true?"* If the answer is still yes, just check in with how you know that. After all, unless you have a crystal ball, if it is something you have not yet tried (or tried at this time), you cannot know exactly how successful you will be.

10th January
Confidence

Yesterday's message was all about releasing the doubt. Today is all about the confidence. When we are starting something new or challenging, we are often waiting to feel confident enough to get going and sometimes that can end up being a very long wait. But you can feel confident right now, in this moment. Think of a time or memory when something went well and you knew you did a good job. Notice the mental movie —what do you see, what do you hear, what do you feel? Now go ahead and notice how your body feels. What are the sensations and where do you feel them in your body? Feeling confident as you are, think about a goal or a project or decision that you have been putting off and notice what happens. And you may just (accidentally) start to feel a whole lot surer about that.

11th January
Pleasant Surprises

Do you like surprises? Most of us would immediately respond with a definite *"yes"*— but probably as long as we knew it was a pleasant surprise! Whilst there are indeed many pleasant surprises to be had, sometimes life throws us a curve ball that we are less than chuffed about. But even those unexpected and seemingly unwanted surprises can be a really good thing. Maybe you can remember a time when you had an experience that seemed less than positive at the time, which turned out to be one of the best things to ever happen. Perhaps a relationship ended and then you met your soul mate, a redundancy brought about the perfect career change, or just a switch in plans meant an even better experience. Today, even if you find yourself in the midst of something unwanted, remember, it could turn out to be a surprise—a very pleasant surprise indeed!

12th January
New Body

If part of your New Year plan was to get into physical shape, today may be a good day to review your goals. Are you seeking optimum health, well-being and fitness or are you trying to achieve a body beautiful that lives up to an ideal portrayed by the media? There is nothing wrong with wanting to be in physical shape but all bodies are naturally beautiful and it would be a very dull world if we all looked identical. So just take a moment to check what is most important to you. It's good to ensure that your goals and dreams are taking you in an aligning direction rather than creating even more conflict inside. Perhaps you want to aim for boundless energy, vitality and va-va-voom rather than trying to fit an imaginary type?

13th January
Getting Motivated

Do you ever find it less than easy to motivate yourself to do things? Maybe it is the desire to exercise more and get fitter or to do the less desirable aspects of your work or just to switch off the TV and do something more productive with your time. We often think of motivation as being synonymous with will power—that somehow we have to dig deep, grit our teeth and plow on regardless. But this is doing things the hard way. The fastest way to increase your motivation is to consider how you will be when you have done it. Go there in your mind's eye and imagine what you will be seeing and hearing and how you will be feeling when it is complete. Your energy will naturally increase and you may just suddenly find yourself mid-task without even having to think about it.

14th January
Opportunities

Life is a continual stream of opportunities. If you are not (yet) experiencing this flow in your life, opportunities may well be happening but you aren't noticing them as they arise. Our focus tends to be quite narrow. Particularly as we get older, we are locked into habits and patterns of thinking confined to our current experiences. Day-to-day, we simply do what needs to be done, just occasionally thinking about future plans. But if we are frank and honest with ourselves, how much of our time do we actually spend visioning our dreams? When a lucky break comes along, our attention is just locked on to what is right in front of us and so the opportunity just flies past completely unnoticed. The good news is that a simple shift in our awareness has a profound impact. We just need to be willing to step back and look up from our daily lives. Then we get to notice all of the boundless possibilities that surround us every day.

15th January
Your Support Crew

Do you have a support crew? Who are the people that you can share your dreams and frustrations with that will help you through tough times and cheer you on in the good? Many of us have that *perfectionist* streak—we need to get it right or we need to do it by ourselves. In fact, often the very time that we most need assistance, we will pull back and retreat into our cave. But as humans, we are communal beings and we are meant to live and work together. Cutting yourself off from people never works out well and just leads to feelings of isolation. Make sure you know who is in your support crew. Find ways to ask for a hand and to offer your self in service. And if you don't think you have one right now, it is an even better time to reach out to positive and life-affirming people to help and be helped along this life journey. It's much more fun to travel with companionship.

16th January
Thoughts We Keep Thinking

Today the JoyScope invites you to play a *thought game*. You may already know that what you repeatedly think about, you create and you therefore become. But did you know that on average we think 60,000 thoughts a day and 98-99% of those thoughts were the same as the thoughts we had yesterday and the day before that and the day before that and so on? So if you want to play the thought game, it is time to bring more conscious processing to your thinking. At regular intervals during the day simply ask yourself what you have been paying attention to. You can even set a timer or an alarm to prompt you into awareness. When you play the game, you may be shocked at how often your attention has drifted onto unhelpful or pointless thoughts. Find a way to change those thoughts to something that inspires you and notice how quickly life begins to change.

17th January
Embracing Uncertainty

We can't predict the future. As much as we would sometimes like to think that we know what will happen, the very nature of being human is that everything remains uncertain. When we feel the desire to see what is coming, it most often comes from a need to control events and people around us. That need always stems from fear and insecurity. But what if your faith comes not from knowing what will happen but through the absolute and unwavering trust that whatever happens in your life that you will be able to handle it? Believing in our ability to respond well to any situation, rather than trying to manage our outer world, gives us complete security. Let go and live freely today knowing that it will all work out. Beyond letting go, there is a whole new level of control!

18th January
But-out!

The message today is to *but-out*! Our choice of language has a powerful impact on people around us. Whenever we disagree with someone or need to offer feedback, we will tend to use the word *but*. For example, *"I can see where you are going with that idea, but this one is better"*. The word *but* is challenging by nature. Even though we may be speaking in very positive terms initially, people will only focus on the bit that comes after *but*. Why not try the word *and* instead. *And* is inclusive and sustains agreement with the other party, *"I can see where you are going with that idea, and this one is even better"*. It builds rapport and fosters harmonious relationships. So forget the *buts* today and focus on *ands*—see how many people you can win over!

19th January
Indulgence

What feels like pure indulgence to you? It could be taking a day off work for some *me-time* or a pyjama day, having a spa or pamper day or buying tickets for an event or experience you have always longed for! Today the JoyScope wants you to give yourself permission to treat *you* in a special way. When we indulge ourselves, we send a message to the Universe that we recognise our worthiness and in doing so, send a clear invitation to others to do the same. So what do you deserve today? Permission granted to treat you!

20th January
Finding Rainbows

As the story goes, at the foot of a rainbow you will find a pot of gold. Of course, the challenge is finding the foot of the rainbow, which is ever-moving and changing. But the real problem is when we become attached to finding the gold and so focus on seeking the foot of the rainbow to the exclusion of everything else. Can anyone fail to be amazed by the beauty of a rainbow in its full and glorious technicolour? Yet we can miss its awe if we have our eyes firmly fixed on finding its foot. So today the JoyScope invites you to look upwards and notice everything that you have been missing. Rather than focus purely on getting to a certain point, just expand your awareness and allow the magnificence of life to take your breath away.

21st January
Planning

Don't you just love it when a plan comes together? Doesn't it feel wonderful when everything just seems to fall into place? Would you like more of those experiences? The good news is that it has very little to do with anything in our outer world. When we centre ourselves, get really clear about what we want and then align ourselves with our desires, Universal energy responds accordingly. That is when we get to experience all of our plans working out effortlessly. Today remember that your work is not about making things happen, your work is about aligning with what you want and allowing the Universe to bring things to fruition. How much easier is that? Have an enjoyable and effortless day!

22nd January
Ceilings

Today the message from the JoyScope is to raise your expectations of what is possible. Any time we perceive there is a ceiling on what we can have, whether in our professional or personal lives, we hold ourselves back. But if the ceiling is only ever a perspective we hold inside us, we can choose to breakthrough to whatever we want. So consider what is on the other side of your self-limitations. If you truly knew that *anything is possible*, what would you choose? Expand your perspective and relish your new viewpoint. When you take away the ceiling, you get to be closer to the stars.

23rd January
Resilience

We are more resilient than we often give ourselves credit for. When you consider all the hardships and struggles that the human race is able to survive, we realise how resourceful people can be. It is true that no one should ever have to suffer. However, it is more often the fear of what might happen that causes us the most angst and emotional turmoil. Nothing will ever happen that you can't handle. Every challenge will help you to tap into the depth of your resourcefulness and bring with it even more insight of the real you. You will continue to learn and grow. At these times, remember that the Universe already knows what you are capable of and trusts you enough to challenge you in this way. Find peace in the awareness of your own greatness.

24th January
Detachment

Whenever we try to hold onto anything, the natural laws of the Universe mean that the thing we want to keep is very likely to slip through our fingers. That is equally true whether that is something physical like money or material goods, something less tangible such as a relationship or job or something more emotional like a state of mind or mood. Once we decide that it has to be a certain way, we have become attached and all of our energy is consumed with trying to sustain it, which inevitably fails. Instead, when we understand that everything will have its natural phases, we can be peacefully at ease with allowing the good stuff to come to us without being dependent on it for our happiness. Everything will continue to come and go. Our joy comes from simply staying present to life.

25th January
More Please!

Every experience can be an opportunity to get more of what we want! When we flow appreciation and gratitude when something good is happening, we affirm to the Universe, "*Yes, more of this please!*" Even when the not-so-good things occur, we can use the situation to our advantage. You see, in moments of contrast, we have the opportunity to make better distinctions about what we want. Don't you know with more clarity what you desire when you are experiencing the exact opposite? For example, you have a head cold or other physical ailment and you *know* you want wellbeing instead. You don't have enough money to pay a bill and you *know* you want abundance and prosperity. The trick is to briefly experience contrast and then immediately focus on what you want instead to bring it into your experience. Try it today and notice how good it feels to be the master of turnarounds.

26th January
Making Decisions

From time to time, life will present us with opportunities or choice points. Sometimes it is easy to know what to do but at other times it can be a challenge to know what to pick. We may even have conflicting desires and dreams and we therefore need time to reflect on the situation. In fact, any time we are finding it less than easy to reach a decision, it is usually because we don't yet have enough information to know what is right for us. Instead of forcing the issue, give yourself time and space to allow the perfect choice to emerge. Repeat the mantra *"I am in the process of deciding"* and be gentle and kind with yourself. Taking time can make all the difference in the world.

27th January
Patience

The saying goes that patience is a virtue. It is certainly true that if we believe that we need things to happen urgently, our desperation will hold us apart from what we want. Any impatience increases our resistance to the natural flow of life and we find ourselves blocking our own dreams. But what we perceive as patience can have very different qualities. We may equate patience with waiting yet when we are in waiting mode, our attention is still fixed on the absence of what we want and so we create more of the same—more waiting! But when we live from a place of joyful expectation, not only are we inviting wonderful events into our lives but we also get as much enjoyment from relishing the whole experience of giddy anticipation. Why not expect to have a wonderful day just for the fun of it?

28th January
Sensitivity

Sensitivity is often frowned upon in Western culture. People who show this quality are advised to *"be strong"*, *"toughen up"* or *"stand up for themselves"*. What an interesting idea! Sensitivity is actually a form of intuition. It is the ability to be highly aware and in tune with our own emotions and to the feelings of others, even when they are unexpressed. The trouble isn't our sensitive nature but rather that we aren't taught how to nurture and hone this skill so that it can be a positive force in our lives. Often we struggle to make peace with an inner quality that also brings complications. It is difficult to follow our own journeys or to make decisions that affect other people when we are so attuned to their emotions. Wouldn't it be wonderful if *sensitivity classes* were taught alongside Maths, History and English at school! Imagine how different the world would be if this was a core subject that we learnt when we were young. Instead of denying your sensitive nature, let's celebrate it. Our attempts to deny and escape it serve no one, and ultimately carry us too far from home. Embrace who you are today and use your magical quality to reach out to others. The world needs more sensitivity!

※

29th January
Special Days

There are certain special days of the year that we celebrate. We mark out birthdays, anniversaries, Valentine's Day and festive holidays. We exchange gifts or tokens of our love and we get together with friends and family to honour the occasion. But what if every day was a cause to celebrate? If we appreciate the miracles that occur each day such as beautiful sunrises, a two-hundred year old oak tree and the sea-creatures that live in the depths of the dark oceans, we can make every day a special day. So what title will you give this day? Appreciation day? Awesome day? The joy-of-living-day? You get to choose how you want to make today count.

※

30th January
Being a Genius

Have you ever considered yourself to be a genius? If your answer is no then you are short-changing yourself. Maybe you have a host of reasons to discount this idea. You didn't get good grades at school, you flunked tests or exams, you struggle to understand intellectual concepts or theories, you haven't invented anything new, you don't have letters after your name or a glittering CV. Some or all of these may appear to be true but they still don't justify your self-limiting thoughts. Why? Because each and every one of us has been gifted with the most amazing mind. And it is not just our mind that we have access to. Beyond all that our reality-focused self can comprehend, lies a universe of inter-connected thoughts, concepts and ideas. If you have ever wondered where a deeply insightful awareness or spark of creative inspiration has miraculously appeared from then perhaps you already know the truth. Today embrace the genius that you are. Expand your horizons and get out of your own way to discover this inspirational flow. The only credible evidence you will ever need is your own direct experience. Now that is a genius idea worth exploring.

31st January
Forgiveness

The theme for today is forgiveness. When you hold onto any blame or anger towards another, the only person who really suffers is you. Our hearts become closed so we can no longer let the good stuff in. So, today, let go of any old hurt and resentment that is no longer serving you. Remember, that whatever the circumstances, people are always doing the best they can at the time. No one would ever deliberately hurt another person from a good and happy place so they must have been out of sorts at the time. More importantly remember that you cannot extend forgiveness to another without forgiving yourself first. So whom do you need to forgive? Go on—set yourself free today!

1st February
Check-in (1)

It may seem that January has flown by. Today is the first day of February. Did you set any goals and intentions for this year? If so, how are you getting on? A new year is a great time for making decisions on what is important and resolving to make changes to bring more of what you want. But it doesn't have to be the first day of January that you make a start. Even if you didn't decide to make any changes at New Year or if your good intentions have slipped, you can still make decisions today (and every day) that line you up with what you want. So what do you choose today?

2nd February
Reasons to Be Happy

Today, your mission is to look for reasons to feel good. Happiness isn't dependent on our life circumstances being *right*. Happiness is the willingness to look beyond the imperfections simply to squeeze the juice out of life. Reasons to smile come in lots of different guises—a child laughing, breath-taking scenery, a good joke—the list is huge! You get to be the architect of your own happiness by designing the moments that feel good. So what will be your reasons? Find one or ten or one hundred today. Of course the *consequence* of pure happiness is that you accidentally radiate smiles. Just notice how they come back to you amplified and then you can add that to your list of reasons to be happy as well.

3rd February
Worthiness

Do you know that you were born whole, happy and complete? Your worthiness has never been and never will be under question. To whom are you trying to prove your worthiness—your parents, your peers or some higher power? The person who usually needs the most convincing is you! If you truly embrace your inner perfection, how would life be different for you? When you stop expecting to know the answer or to get it right, doesn't that bring you so much more peace? How much more joy, love and abundance do you experience when you hold yourself in the highest regard? How much more do you then have available to give to others? Today treat yourself with the kindness and respect that you deserve.

4th February
Expanding Relationships

Are you willing to expand your relationships? When we are in a relationship, whether intimate, family, professional or friendship, we tend to have certain expectations about the other person. We may believe positive aspects such as they are genuine and loving or we may believe less positive things like they are unreasonable and unfair. But when we label another person a specific way, our judgments limit the experiences we can have with them. In fact, they cannot behave any differently to our perception of them! That is why we can think kind thoughts and bring out the best in a person or find ourselves in conflict when we think less positively. If you want to have better relationships, the fastest approach is to expand your expectations of who they are. When we believe that everyone is doing the best they can and supporting our highest and best interests at all times, we transform our relationships.

5th February
Unlimited Language

The way that we use our language has a direct impact on our life. Today notice any of the ways in which you limit the amount of joy in your life by what you say. The good news is that some small adjustments can make a really big difference. When we say, *"This is going to be difficult"*, we stop the experience from being anything else but tough. Like the genie in the lamp, our subconscious mind hears our thoughts and says, *"Your wish is my command, difficult it shall be!"* But when you use your language to orientate yourself to what you want, it can be transformational. What if instead you say, *"This may be less than easy"*? This time your genie hears easy and thinks, *"Easy it shall be!"* And of course, if you really wanted to have fun with this, you could always say something like *"This is sure to be a lot easier than I am currently thinking"*! Today is a great day to play with how you use your words. Focus more on what you want and use your language to reflect the direction in which you want to go.

6th February
Environment

How we feel about our surrounding environment really matters. Both at work and at home, our habitat will either be soul nourishing and uplifting or depleting valuable energy and well-being. Whether or not you live in your dream house or work in a perfect workspace, some small changes can have a profound impact. What can you add to make your environment more inspiring? Well, good lighting is essential, especially in the darker months. Natural daylight is perfect but if that is not available, you can buy lightbulbs that mimic the natural light of the sun. A few strategically placed lamps can work wonders. Bringing nature inside can also help. Cut flowers or a plant pot brighten any environment. Even if you are limited by what you can add to your space, little mementos or photographs can remind you of good times and reactivate all of those feel-good vibrations! Why not even go all out and create a little altar or reflection space of your favourite things. Make your space work for you.

7th February
A Comforting Word

Sometimes we all just need a bit of reassurance. A comforting word that lets us know that things will all work out in the end. The JoyScope has seen your future and wants to let you know that *it is all going to be okay*. Let go of all your concerns and worries. It simply drains your energy when you are focusing on things that may happen and anticipating the worst. Instead, keep your focus firmly on where you are headed. Only tackle the issues that are real and present and even then, only if they have significance. Otherwise let go, let go, let go! Give yourself the gift of emotional freedom today.

8th February
Choose Your Response

We aren't in control of other people's behaviours or actions but we are in control of our reactions! Today you are invited to choose your responses. If you feel people are passing judgments unfairly, know that is simply their opinion. Everyone has their own unique perspective and that is their prerogative. Does what they are saying inspire you or provide you with constructive feedback that supports your personal growth? If not, let it go and free yourself. If someone acts in a way that you find aggravating or upsetting, consider what the real impact is. Often their act is done and dusted fairly quickly but we drag it out by continually replaying it or discussing it rather than simply moving on. Be the one who moves gently through your life today and let go of any reactions that aren't in your own highest and best interests.

9th February
Self-respect

How would you feel if you were one of the most respected people in the world? Knowing that we are respected boosts our self-esteem and confidence. So are you interested in the fastest way to gain respect? Give it to yourself in abundance. Treat yourself with the respect you deserve. Hold yourself to standards of excellence and give of your best. And sometimes, if the best doesn't seem to be quite enough, rather than berating yourself, be gentle, kind and loving. When we have complete respect for ourselves, we invite others to treat us in the same way and we are more generous with our respect for others too. And that makes the world a better place to be!

10th February
Generosity

Do you consider yourself to be a generous person? Maybe you are the first to dip your hand in your pocket for a worthwhile cause? Perhaps you like to give lavish gifts on birthdays and other special occasions? Or you are willing to lend money or items to people when they need them most? But do you give generously of yourself? Are you able to be fully present in conversation without your mind wandering onto other topics or what you want to be saying next? Can you be a shoulder to cry on without needing to try and problem-solve or fix the other person? Can you care for another person (a sick child, partner or parent perhaps) without feeling anxious or resentful about all the other things you could or should be doing? There is no judgment here, just awareness that the greatest gift we can ever give is our presence with kindness, openness and grace. Generosity is not in the things we do; it is a state of being that gently holds the world in the arms of love.

11th February
Starting Your Day

Do you find yourself starting the day contemplating your to-do list? Perhaps you begin by running a mental movie of everything that needs to be done, all the places you need to be, conversations and meetings that need to be held and so on. Do you give yourself the gift of also considering how you want to be feeling as you are going through your day? Usually we get so focused on the action part of our journey that we don't take the time or space to reflect on how we want to be as a person *living our day*. If we haven't pre-paved the experiences we want to have, we are really relying on a hit and miss approach. Maybe we will be lucky and be in the right (emotional) place at the right time or maybe not. Do you want to leave it to chance? Instead, we can spend a little more time finding ways to feel good. It may seem as though you are too busy to take time out but as our emotional state will dictate our productivity and success anyway, you haven't really got time not to!

12th February
Immersion Experiences

Are you ready to totally enjoy your life? If you want to bask in the good times, you need to fully immerse yourself in the experience. In a cautious world, we may find ourselves dipping a toe in the water at the edge of the pool but how can we ever hope to discover the real experience unless we are prepared to jump right in? We discount too many possibilities when we haven't had the full immersion experience. We hold back on a first date and then declare they weren't entertaining or engaging enough. We give up on a new hobby or skill before we have experienced the first hints of mastery. We dismiss opportunities during preliminary discussions without ever diving in and exploring the depths of what could be possible. So make a decision today to be the one that allows more than a toe to get wet. Only by being fully immersed can you ever discover the truth.

13th February
Authenticity

Today the message from the JoyScope is a reminder to *all ways* be yourself. When we try to shape ourselves to meet the expectations of others, we end up losing our sense of who we really are. What others think and feel becomes more important than the intuitive hunches and guidance we receive on the inside. Authenticity is a willingness to show up and just be you, no matter what. We are all perfect just as we are and there is no need to *pretend* to be someone or something that we are not. It's okay to believe what you believe, to know what you know and to feel what you feel. You are not required to do or be anything else—The Universe loves you just the way you are. So just relax into knowing your own worth and enjoy being the real you.

14th February
Valentine's Vibe

Like it or loathe it, here in the UK it is difficult to escape the Valentine's vibe. Maybe you are a big fan and ready to celebrate in style or maybe you would rather escape from the hype to anywhere else. Either way, when there is love in the air, it can be completely contagious! So whom do you love and who needs to hear it? If you have been married for a while, perhaps you can think back to the excitement of your wedding day and remind your spouse of the vows you took. If you are in a newer relationship, you may look to connect on an even deeper level. If you are single and ready to meet The One, this is an opportunity to revel in the good feelings, knowing that as you do, you call that special person into your life. If you are happy flying solo then reflect on the people you love most and make sure they know it! You are loving to the absolute core of your being. So, whatever your situation, be the person who spreads love and joy today.

15th February
Conscious Decisions

Today is going to be a great day for you. You may be asking how can I know that when I may not even know you or your personal circumstances? Have you ever found yourself making the decision that it is going to be a *not-so-great* day based on the external evidence you have gathered? For example, you get out of bed and stub your toe, spill toothpaste on your black clothes, find yourself running late and then get stuck in a traffic jam and think to yourself, "*It's going to be one of those days!*" Ever noticed that from that point on, you get to be right and the day doesn't turn out so well. There will always be evidence to support that it is a good or a bad day. We just have to choose which way we want to focus. So the message from the JoyScope is that it *is* going to be one of those days today. It is going to be a day packed to the brim with excitement, inspiration, connection, passion and fun. Today collect evidence to support this claim. Your mission, if you choose to accept it, is to prove the JoyScope right.

16th February
Both Ends of the Stick

When we pick up a stick, we pick up both ends. Life is exactly the same. In every moment there is wanted and unwanted. If you want a life that is full of passion and inspiration then there are also going to be times of emotional disharmony and disappointment. If you want a life that is fast moving and exciting then there are also going to be times when you hit a bump in the road. If you want a full and rich life experience then there will also be times when you will feel overwhelmed. Our job is to keep our focus on what is wanted. Any time today that you become aware that you are holding the wrong end of the stick and focusing on a problem or issue, just gently remind yourself that there is another end too. What are all the positives that you are not yet noticing?

17th February
Juice

If your life feels a little flat, it may be time for an injection of juice! Routines and systems help to automate our lives and make things run smoothly but when we follow the same patterns day in and day out, we kill off all the enthusiasm and passion that makes life juicy. If your life is feeling less than inspiring, maybe it's time to make a change. If there were no obstacles or blocks, what would you choose instead? If it's a big shift like a change in job or moving house it may not be completely possible (yet) but you can start to consider the options and just exploring ideas can add a little zest to your life. And you never know, there may be just one small thing that you could do today to move you closer to that dream—what would that be?

18th February
Inner Child

Today the JoyScope invites you to reconnect to your inner child. With so much uncertainty and chaos in the world, we are required to be very grown up to cope with life challenges, and our fun and playful sides are often neglected. Today take time to remember all the things you enjoyed doing when you were young. What made your heart and soul sing? Maybe it was climbing a tree, colouring pictures or building castles in a sand pit. It could be anything that comes to mind. The important thing is to give yourself the gift of some time spent playing with your inner child. The benefits are tremendous—a renewal of passion, enthusiasm and vitality in all areas of your life. Go on; let the child that is you out to play today!

19th February
Focus on You

Today the JoyScope wants to remind you of the importance of focus. We live in an era of information overload and if we are not selective it is easy to be left spinning with data. Should we eat this or that, should we say this or that, should we believe this or that? The list is endless! In fact, you often find yourself heading in the direction of whoever happens to be shouting loudest, which is unlikely to be the best way for you. So today bring your focus of attention back to you and your life. Connect to your dreams and desires and don't let anyone or anything sway you from your path. It's your life. It's your time. Make it count!

20th February
Thought Tunes

Do you ever find a song running through your head that you just can't seem to shake off? You may not even particularly like the song but the tune is so catchy that it keeps popping up when you least expect (or want) it. Well the same is true of some of our thoughts and many of these are occurring without us even noticing. Repetitive and unhelpful thoughts are like the subconscious thieves of our energy and well-being. Ever noticed that it is less than easy to try to stop thinking a thought we keep thinking? We can't prevent thoughts; we can only invite new ones instead. So what thoughts would you like to have today? What is the most inspiring, uplifting, thrilling, toe-tingling idea you would like to focus upon? Make those new thoughts your new thought tune and you may just notice that the unhelpful thinking miraculously disappears.

21st February
Cherish Yourself

Do you cherish yourself? Self-care and nurturing are essential components to a happy and inspired life. We cannot be there for other people unless we have made ourselves the number one priority in our own lives. So how can you ensure that you feel cherished? Do you need to put your feet up, chill out and relax? Perhaps it is time to sit down and really listen to what your heart and soul are saying? Maybe you need to remove yourself from difficult or challenging situations that are draining your energy? Start each day with your own statement of intent: *"Today I will cherish myself by _____"* and pick what feels most indulgent and rewarding.

22nd February
New Learning

The message from the JoyScope today is to ignite your passion for learning. Perhaps you didn't enjoy school or even took on negative beliefs about your ability to learn—that you weren't intelligent enough or quick enough or hard-working enough. Remember that these were just conditioned thoughts developed in the face of competition and comparison and filtered through our young and naive minds. Don't allow those out-dated beliefs to hold you back from learning now. Whether it is buying a book or enrolling on a course at night school, finding a new subject to stimulate the mind can be really rewarding. Continuing to expand our comfort zones is a recipe for personal satisfaction and fulfillment. So maybe there is something you have always wanted to learn. Take the first step today and enjoy the success of expanding your horizons.

23rd February
Life's Riches

In our culture of having it all, it can be too easy to focus on the *lack* of what we have. Yet if you are reading this, you must already have more than a large proportion of the world's population, many of whom live in extreme poverty. So the message from the JoyScope today is to take some time to appreciate all you have. Remember that abundance comes in many different forms not just through financial or material gain. You can take stock of your life today, appreciate whatever you have and immediately feel rich. And as you do, you become a channel for even more of what you want to flow to you.

24th February
Creativity

Today the JoyScope invites you to get creative! Creativity is the outlet for our self-expression and comes in many different forms. We may find opportunities to invent, produce, generate or construct in the workplace but the most fulfilling creations are personal projects. So what are you inspired to develop? Do you have green thumbs and could grow your own flowers or veggies? Are you drawn to the arts and would like to draw, paint or sculpt? Maybe you are musical and create through singing or playing an instrument? Are you a little bit crafty and could make cards, jewellery or scrapbooks? Maybe you are the next DIY maestro and ready to turn your house into a show-home of your very best work. Perhaps even the next Jamie Oliver or Nigella Lawson and your creations come in the edible form. The choices are endless but sharing who you are through your projects is a magical process that feeds and nourishes the soul. Express yourself today!

25th February
Analysis Paralysis

Do you ever find yourself over-analysing things? Not the general weighing up of pros and cons but becoming locked in a pattern of needing to comprehend everything to the nth degree? Our ego cleverly disguises our fear of taking action and moving forward and allows us to rationalise this under the heading of *not being ready*! There genuinely may be times when we need more information to be able to make a plan but if you have been stuck in that phase for a while, it could be masked fear blocking your way. That doesn't mean you need to jump into hasty decisions. The good news is that the simplest antidote to getting moving again is to take small steps in any direction. When you just take the smallest next step, it doesn't matter if it doesn't take you where you want to go because you can just sidestep and take another route. As you do, you will start to build some movement and energy into your life and new information to help your decision-making process will reveal itself. It feels so much better to get going. Why not *un-stick* yourself today?

26th February
Stepping Up

There is a famous Gandhi quote, *"Be the change you want to see in the world"*. The power of this statement is that it doesn't ask us to take action. Instead it calls upon us to be all of who we are. We are invited to transcend our limiting thoughts and conditioning and connect to the best of us. This is the time for leaders and role models to step forward. All it requires of us is to hold ourselves to the standards we want to see in the world. Today be the one to step up and be counted. Speak from the heart to those you connect with. Have faith in people and withhold judgments. See the best in everyone and everything. In this simple way, you can make the biggest difference.

27th February
B.L.Q.

What is your big life question (BLQ)? What would you like to discover the answer to whilst you are on this planet? For many of us, the BLQ exists completely unconsciously and plays a big part in the quality of our life. For example, imagine how someone may experience life if they are asking a BLQ such as *"How can I continue to grow and discover more of who I am?"* compared to someone who is asking, *"Why does this have to happen to me?"* One BLQ is orientating you towards what you want, the other focuses in on the problem and keeps you stuck. Today pay conscious attention to the questions that you ask. Notice if they serve and empower you? If not, you can choose a different question. Turn it around and focus on what you do want instead and be amazed at how quickly you notice a difference.

28th February
Saying No

Have you ever found yourself doing something for someone else that you really didn't want to do? Maybe you felt obligated to do it or you took pity on them or maybe you were just too fearful of their response to say *"no".* Have you ever noticed that it doesn't seem to work out that well? You may feel that they weren't grateful or appreciative or it may even backfire completely! When we do something for another person that we aren't aligned with doing, the resistant energy inside of us gets carried into the action and that has a far greater impact that any good will in the action itself. So today, if you find yourself in a position of being asked to do something that you would really rather not, either politely decline or align yourself with doing it by finding the hidden benefits to you. When you support others from a place of generosity and love, it always works out well.

29th February
Your Extra Day

Today is a special day! Usually we have just 365 days in a year but every four years we get an extra day for free. In our fast-paced and hectic lives when time is at a premium, an extra 24 hours is really a blessing. So how will you acknowledge this gift of time? If we just continue to cram even more into our already packed schedules, the day will pass by unnoticed. Instead, take at least a moment to pause and be appreciative of what a little more time can give you. You may still have to go to work or follow a routine but you get to choose how you spend the time in between. Rather than just catching up on chores and obligations, remind yourself that this day is really a special extra and do something out of the ordinary. Why not? Life can always return back to normal again tomorrow—if you wish!

1st March
Spring

Is there a hint of spring in the air? Spring is the time of new beginnings. That which has lain dormant through the winter months, now begins to emerge in amazing and miraculous ways. So what has been lying dormant in you and is ready to emerge? What ideas or insights have you been pondering? What seeds could you be sowing that could flourish and bloom in the coming months? This is a really good time to start projects and make plans. If you could create anything what would it be? Start to tend to your inner garden and watch the *growing* results that follow.

2nd March
Feedback

Do you enjoy receiving feedback? If it is positive and uplifting and reminds us of our magnificence, we are likely to say "*yes!*" If it is critical or less than constructive, we may be less inclined to want it. But feedback is simply the perception someone else has of us. It is their opinion filtered through their lens on the world. So in fact, the way to handle all feedback (positive and negative) is the same. The first step is to just check inside—does it have any resonance? If the comments seem hurtful, it may well be that you already hold that opinion of yourself and the pain comes from tapping into the part you would prefer not to show. In which case, the other person is simply your mirror reflecting the healing work you have not yet done. Even if the comments are overwhelmingly positive, it is still valuable to explore the truth inside you. When we ensure that we use our own reference experiences before accepting other opinions, we create a solid platform in our lives and are able to live authentically and in alignment.

3rd March
Forward Momentum

From time to time we all can feel like we have got a bit stuck on the journey of life. We may have lost sight of what we want or simply not know what to do next or even feel thwarted by events and experiences outside our control. When this happens, we may be inclined to think that the solution needs a big and dramatic change. Although that might happen naturally, often the easiest route is just to introduce some kind of forward momentum into your life. It doesn't have to be big or scary! Often the simplest steps can be the most effective. What is one thing that would move you forwards today? The antidote to stuck-ness is just one step and another and another. Before you know it, you are back on track and flowing through life. Forwards, forwards, forwards!

4th March
Sowing Seeds

When we have wanted something for a long time, our ability to trust that it is on its way into our lives can waver. Like digging up a seed to check it's growth, we look at the evidence in our life (or lack of it) and question whether it can happen. We live in a world of opportunity where anything is possible. Our job is to focus our desire on what we want and then allow it to manifest in our lives. What seeds have you planted? Today the message from JoyScope is to step away and let the seeds grow. Put your attention on all that is working in your life, no matter how small it may seem. Live with pure unwavering faith that whatever you want will happen at the perfect time and in the perfect way. You just get to stand back and watch it grow.

5th March
Divine Grace

Today the JoyScope invites you to widen your intentions. Clarity and concentration can be powerful tools in manifesting our lives. Having laser beam focus when we know what we want can certainly help us to identify the actions that will move us closer to our dreams. The potential downside is that when our focus is too narrow, our intentions can limit rather than inspire us. We demand that the world unfolds in a particular way and when things happen differently we are left feeling like we are lost or late. Try gently softening your perspective today. Make your intention about the feelings and states of being you would like to experience as you go through your day rather than the specifics of events or activities. When we are connected to Divine Grace, the need for clarity and concentration just ebbs away and we find ourselves bouncing beautifully along with the energy of all that is.

6th March
Contentment

It is okay to have big dreams and desires. That is the way that the juice of life flows through us. But usually it is the day-to-day things that bring the most contentment in the moment—A hug from a loved one, the sun shining or the good company of friends. It can really be that simple. Perhaps you can recall a time when a seemingly small thing brought you contentment? So if we want to feel good right now, we only have to spend more time creating those kinds of experiences. And guess what, from that place of contentment, it becomes so much easier to manifest our desires anyway. Truly content whilst dreaming big is the perfect recipe for a happy life!

7th March
Thinking Differently

Today is a really good day for thinking differently. We have a tendency to always examine life from a set perspective. Like a spotlight, we hone in on a particular viewpoint to the exclusion of everything else. Are you ready to change your vantage point? When you consider your life right now, what would be one thing you could easily change or improve that would make the biggest difference? Now imagine what your life would be like having made that change. How would you be feeling knowing you had been successful? What else would you be noticing? From this place, now consider what you will do differently to move you closer to what you really want. Thinking differently is easy when we choose to expand our perspective.

8th March
Filters

Do you want to be right or do you want to be happy? Sometimes we can get locked into self-defeating patterns of behaviour because we think it is more important to get our point across and have someone else accept their liability or wrongness. But perception is personal and always limited.

We are filtering our experience through our own values and beliefs and no two people will ever filter in exactly the same way. Why not let go of the need to be right this week? When we allow another (even when they are disallowing us), amazing things can happen. You may find a common ground that you never knew you had.

9th March
Be Love

The message from the JoyScope today is to let the love flow! We can get hooked up in the busyness of day-to-day life and forget to tell the people we care about what they mean to us. A few simple words of acknowledgment go a really long way and the benefits are always reciprocal. And of course, if you are showering people with appreciation, there is that one person who needs extra special recognition—you! After all, it's only you who is with yourself every step of this journey from beginning to end and that is quite a commitment. So go ahead and love yourself. Love your friends and family. Love everyone. Just be… love!

10th March
Interdependence

Do you consider yourself to be independent? It's good to be able to take care of yourself. To be logistically and emotionally self-sufficient creates a sense of freedom. But there is a downside. When everyone is acting independently, community and social cooperation break down and we lose that sense of connection. There is another way.

Beyond independence there is inter-dependence. That is a willingness to take care of your own needs whilst supporting others. And it is equally important to be able to ask for help when you need it. In doing so, you allow others to share the best of themselves too. How can you become a co-creator today?

11th March
Twists and Turns

Plans are great when it all works out. It's not quite so much fun when those plans go belly up. We may feel frustrated, upset or angry when things don't seem to be going our way. The trouble with twists and turns is that they have a nasty habit of obscuring our view. What we most desire may be just around the next corner whilst we are frozen to the spot lamenting our broken dreams. Are you willing to carry on with your journey regardless of what appears to be happening? Take a peek around the next corner and see what lies in store for you. There may be another curve or bend for you to navigate or maybe you will discover something unexpected. Sometimes the twists and turns actually turn out to be better than the original plan.

12th March
Living on Purpose

Does your life have purpose? When we live a life with meaning and direction, we are naturally motivated to move towards things and people that inspire us. Rather than dragging ourselves out of bed in the morning, we can rise effortlessly with the desire to fulfill our intentions. Of course, it can be wonderful to have a sense of a life mission to be the guiding star on our path. Yet when we become so focused on trying to discover what we are here to be and do, we miss the many miraculous moments that are already happening right now. In fact, every aspect of our life can generate reasons to live *on purpose* —the work we do, raising children, creating outstanding relationships, our passions and hobbies. When you live on and with purpose, you strengthen your commitment to your life and that is where the magic happens.

13th March
Records of Life

What records of your life do you keep? Maybe you have a journal? Or do you take photographs or collect keepsakes of memories? Or perhaps you blog about your experiences? Maybe you think that you aren't recording anything? But what about in your mind's eye? Our minds are like filing systems that store all the data about our lives and present relevant evidence as we ask for it. And we get what we ask for! Want more evidence that it is a scary and hostile world? Your mind has files to offer on that. Want proof that life is unfair? Your mind can show you reasons to believe that too. Want to build a case against that person as being mean or hurtful? Guess what, there is confirmation of that too! But it works the other way as well. So what files are you going to open today? The files labeled fear or the ones to do with love, joy, happiness, kindness, trust and faith? All the files exist but you get to choose where to look!

14th March
Achievements

Today is about recognising your achievements. What has been your greatest accomplishment? What are you most proud of? Where have you excelled in life? In this fast-paced world, more often that not, we are on to the next thing without really taking the time to register and mark our successes. Today's challenge is to compile a list of your greatest accomplishments. How many can you find? When you think you are done, stretch yourself to find even more. Not only is the process positively addictive but you also solidify your self-esteem and self-belief—then you can add that to your list of accomplishments too!

15th March
Putting You First

We all want to make a difference in the world. Maybe we want to leave a legacy after we have gone or maybe it is simply being a force for good in the lives of those close to us. And it's good to have those inspirational intentions. Where it can get complicated is when we try to be there for everyone else and neglect to take care of ourselves. That is when contribution becomes obligation and that just leads to festering resentment, stress and eventual burnout. When we put our own needs first, step up and take responsibility for our own well-being, we are much better placed to support and care for those around us. When our cup runneth over with feel-good energy and vitality then we get to share that with the world and that makes the biggest difference.

16th March
Back to the Future

Today the JoyScope wants to take you on a journey. Climb aboard the time machine whilst we travel back through your life. As we travel back, notice all of those memories and events that have been part of your path—all of those experiences that have made you the amazing person that you are today. Now through the magic of time travel, we are going to visit your future. Can you see all of the wonderful experiences that the Universe is lining up for you? We travel on to a point in your future where you are sitting in your rocking chair by a warming fire watching the last embers die down and reflecting on the incredible life you led. Doesn't it feel wonderful to know you fulfilled your potential? With all of that warmth in your heart and soul, return to now, remembering the wonders that life has in store for you.

17th March
Maintaining Momentum

It's at this time of year that we can lose some of the motivation that comes with the start of a fresh year. So if you want to keep the momentum going, how do you access the right mindset day in and day out? Well it could be a lot easier than you think. Just notice what you were thinking at New Year! We usually have a whole belief system that inspires us to make changes, such as *"it's a fresh start"* or *"this will* be my year" or "*this year, I'm going to achieve _____* ". Any time our motivation slips, we have just changed our thoughts, usually in response to things not working out quite as we would want. So if you want to re-motivate yourself, just find a new thought that gets you going again—"*it's never too late to have a great year*", "*I've already learnt what doesn't work, now I can focus on what does*" or "*every day I am moving closer to my dreams*". Find the words that uplift and inspire you and you really will have your best year yet.

18th March
Finding Focus

Our minds function best when focused on just one thing. At an absolute stretch we can hold about three to four thoughts in our head at once. Yet how many of us try to think through multiple ideas, decisions and problems at the same time. Simple decisions, like choosing what to eat for lunch, use up our limited source of brain-power so imagine what handling complex projects does to your mental energy supply. So the message from the JoyScope today is to keep your focus. Gently request of yourself and your mind that irrelevant thoughts and ideas stay out of difficult mental processing tasks so that you can focus on what is really important. You will notice that you free up essential energy and therefore become much more productive.

19th March
Date Yourself

Today the JoyScope would like you to plan a date! This is a very different kind of date because the person you get to spend some quality time with is *you*! Pick a day or evening in your diary and set aside all the people, projects and demands, and plan the perfect time just for you. When you think back to one of the best dates you ever had, didn't you make an extra effort? Didn't you consider what would make it particularly special? Didn't you ensure that you treated the other person with respect and kindness? The same applies to this date. Make it your dream date in whatever way feels right—picking the perfect venue, turning off your phone or pager, treating and pampering yourself. Dating ourselves is a powerful way to build a strong and solid inner relationship that makes coping with the usual stresses and strains a breeze. You may find you even want to make it a regular occurrence in your schedule.

20th March
Symbolic Meaning

Most of us will readily accept the idea that our dreams contain symbols and messages but if we believe that we create our own reality by our unconscious thoughts then it would also be true that our daily lives can have symbolic meaning too. This is not to suggest that we should read meaning into every small event (we would never get anything done!) but it can be useful to interpret themes that seem to be running through our lives. For example, colds and runny nose, leaking pipes or floods can all be symbols of unreleased emotion. If you notice certain patterns emerging, it is beneficial to ask what it could mean if it was a message from the Divine. The key to doing this effectively is to stay in a place of openness to the meaning, taking responsibility rather than blame for what is occurring. This fosters a deeper connection with our infinitely wise Higher Self and creates more awareness and choice about how we live our lives.

21st March
Road Love

Road rage seems to have become one of the norms of our culture today. Something changes when we climb in those boxes on wheels that simply wouldn't happen if we were walking down the street. Anyone who has been on the receiving end of any kind of road-based anger (even if it is just those not-so-supportive gestures when you are perceived as doing something wrong) knows the impact it can have. The truth is that road rage is simply an outlet for the general frustrations and irritations happening in other areas of their lives. It isn't the action that angers them; it is the meaning they make of it. For example, someone cuts in front of their car and they react to the feelings in their life of being unacknowledged or insignificant. When we understand that, we have the opportunity to respond differently. Instead of reacting or retaliating we can stay centred and send blessings. An acknowledging nod and a wave is often the perfect antidote to road rage. Imagine how much more fun driving would become if we all practised the art of road love!

22nd March
Loving Vibes

The quality of our life is always a direct reflection of the quality of our relationships. The inherent nature of being human is that we thrive through relationship with others. Research has proved that love and affection are as fundamental as food and shelter to the survival of babies. When we are in love, everything in life seems to improve. Those issues and niggles that were really bothersome before, no longer affect us. And here is the good news—you can choose to be in love at any time! When we fall for someone, we naturally focus on all their positive qualities (and filter out anything we find less appealing!) So if you want to have those loved-up vibes today, pick someone to think only positive thoughts about—whether it is your partner, a friend or your child, love them unconditionally today and let the good feelings rush in.

23rd March
Milestones

Have you noticed that sometimes the best-laid plans don't always work out in the way you want? That's usually because we are trying to put things in place to ensure that life unfolds in a particular way. But you may be beginning to realise that we don't live in a certain world. In fact, rather than finding the certainty we seek, we often make life even more complex when we try to restrict the natural flow. Instead of making detailed plans, it is much more effective to use milestones. First identify what you want and your reasons for having it. Make sure your outcome feels exciting and inspiring. Then simply identify the key steps that you want to happen along the way. You don't need to know the specifics of when and where, they should just feel as exciting as your final goal. As you reach each milestone give yourself permission to celebrate knowing that you are moving ever closer to your dreams!

24th March
Step-back Day

When was the last time you had a *step-back* day? A step-back day is an opportunity for you to take stock of your life. You pull your attention back from the world, from the people and the projects that *need* your attention and focus just on you. You can ask yourself what you most want and need to live an inspired life? You can explore options and opportunities. You can play with ideas. You can act as if every dream is not just possible but totally inevitable! When do you really take the time to do that? There are so many demands on our time and mindless distractions that we may never find the space. So schedule a step-back day and allow the inspiration to strike.

25th March
Positive Indecision

In this fast-paced world, we are regularly required to reach conclusions and make decisions quickly. Led by the business world, where seizing opportunities is seen as paramount to success, this approach has seeped into our personal lives as well. But making a rapid decision is not always the best thing. Once we have reached a decision, we have ruled out all other possibilities. Our soul loves having time to mull things over and often there may be another option or solution that we haven't yet considered—it could even be so much better than our first thought! Today give yourself time to ponder and muse before reaching a conclusion. You may just get to be pleasantly surprised by what emerges.

26th March
Breath-taking Beauty

We live in a beautiful world. It can be a little too easy to forget that sometimes. But when you consider all of the diversity—the magnificence of mountains, the richness of the greenery, the endless sand hills of deserts, the deep blue seas and oceans—doesn't it just take your breath away? It may seem like the world is in turmoil with epidemics, environmental and economical disasters but underneath all of that, the perfection of the Universe is always ever present. We can choose to focus on the doom and gloom or instead turn our attention to all that is good. Worrying and angst solves nothing. When we flood the world with appreciation for everything and everyone, we make the greatest contribution. Step outside today and take in the beauty of the world. Be a *Universe-appreciator*!

27th March
Self-belief

Do you believe in yourself? Is it strong belief? Is it unquestionable, unshakable, pure and positive belief that you can achieve anything your heart desires and you put your mind to. Self-belief makes anything and everything seem possible. And to be frank, if you are not believing in and supporting yourself, how can you ask or expect anyone else to either. Make today the day that you decide to give yourself the gift of unwavering self-belief. Notice how the day unfolds when you are cheering yourself onwards and upwards. Notice how much more you can get done. Notice how much easier those challenges seem to get. Notice how much more appreciative you become. Notice how much more fun and enjoyment you can have in life. Sounds appealing? Go on, you can do it—believe in *you*!

28th March
Stop the Treadmill

The basis of life is freedom. Isn't that amazing? We live in a universe where, moment-by-moment, we get to choose. We have unlimited options around what we do, what we have and what we want to be. When life gets busy, we may find it less than easy to remember that we are always making choices. Sometimes we can feel that we are on a treadmill and getting nowhere fast. So today the JoyScope reminds you that it is *your* treadmill and you can push the *stop* button whenever you would like. Why not stop and pause, take a deep breath and reconnect to your freedom. It's your life. It's your day! What do you choose?

29th March
Yin and Yang

There are two aspects to our persona. We all possess the masculine energy (yang) and feminine energy (yin) to various degrees. Even though we label these energies as masculine and feminine, it does not mean that men have more yang and women more yin as they co-exist within us all. In fact, these energies can shift and change inside us depending on internal and external triggers. In the last part of the 20th Century, the culture of *having it all* invited us all into our yang. That is the energy that drives us to achieve results and get things done. Now we are being asked to reconnect to our yin energy to bring our bodies and our communities back into balance. Yin helps us to connect more fully to each other, to build co-creative relationships and has a gentle and nurturing quality. Whether you are male or female, today is a good day to tap into your yin energy. How can you be more loving and kind to you and those around you today? As you do, your life will come into balance with greater ease and flow.

30th March
Creative Force

How do you feel when inspiration strikes? It is like a deep breath of life that awakens our souls and opens our eyes to what is possible. If you would like to experience more uplifting moments today, you simply need to tap into your inspiration. And it can be easier than we think. Inspiration adores space. It is a creative power that appears when we are just moodling and pottering and dawdling along. When our minds are peaceful and we let go of our need to always know the answer, that is when this creative force surges through us. So find time today to be busy doing very little and you may just get to be delightfully surprised by the insights you get.

31st March
Flexibility

We all need some flexibility in life. Flexibility is when we are able to respond to life as it happens—to roll with the punches and to seize the opportunities as they happen. When we are too hung up on things going a certain way, we become rigid. Our expectations limit the possibilities in our life. When we have an idea of what we would like without being attached to the form it takes, we give the Universe the scope to deliver the absolute best solution. So would you prefer to rely on your own narrow perspective to work out what you really need or to let the all-knowing, all-seeing, expansive, all-that-there-is source of creation decide? I think we know the answer. Stay flexible!

1st April
April Fooling

It's April Fools Day and that's a great day for getting up to mischief. So are you up for a game? Your challenge, should you choose to accept it, is to make as many people smile as you can. And you've got to keep count too! You can do whatever it takes—a simple smile at your victim through to a full-blown, sidesplitting, tears-running-down-their-face joke. The choice is yours! Don't let anyone get away from you today without some of your positivity rubbing off on them. Smiling is contagious so your task should actually be easy—the plus side is that not only does it make you and them feel good but when you walk around with a permanent inane grin on your face, it generally makes people wonder what you've been up to and that is a whole lot of fun. Enjoy fooling around today!

2nd April
Luck

This is a particularly *lucky* day! So how do you want to use it? If you believed that statement to be true and you knew that success was the only option, what would you do? Would you apply for your dream job or a promotion or ask for a pay rise? Or would you take that first step towards starting your own business or new project? Would you join a dating agency or ask *that* special person out on a date? Would you sign up for a new challenge—a night school course, a marathon or a sky dive? Beliefs are self-fulfilling in nature so the invitation from the JoyScope today is to believe in your own good fortune. When you *know* you are lucky, you *all ways* get to be right!

3rd April
Move Your Body

You may have heard the expression, "*Move your body, move your mind*". When we find ourselves stuck on a problem, facing a challenge or with creativity blocks, then rather than struggling on, we are better advised to get moving! Take a break and do some exercise—go for a walk, a dip in the pool or pick up a tennis racquet. Whilst you are focused on moving your body and enhancing your well-being, your mind can work through other things behind the scenes. Not only will you have renewed energy and vitality, you may well experience more of those insightful a-ha moments when you get back to the original challenge.

4th April
Home Business

Today the JoyScope asks, "*Whose business are you in*?" The wonderful Byron Katie coined the phrase as a way of highlighting how we cause hurt and suffering in our own lives by focusing too much on what other people are doing. And when we are locked into our judgments or opinions on the rightness or wrongness of someone else's behaviour, we don't have the focus (or energy) on our own lives or on taking inspired action that lines us up with our dreams and desires. So today, you are invited to notice when you have your attention on someone else, and to then gently remind yourself to come home to you. It is true that home is where the heart is. It's your heart. It's your life. Take care of home business!

5th April
Abundance

We live in an abundant universe. There is an infinite supply of whatever we want. The people who thrive in economically uncertain times are the people who stay out of scarcity mentality and trust the natural flow of prosperity in life. It isn't always the easiest viewpoint to adopt when the evidence around us suggests otherwise but if we keep our focus on what we want, we allow the gifts of the Universe to find us. That may come in the shape of a windfall or salary increase but often it appears in our life in less tangible ways (for example, vouchers or discounts on our shopping!). To increase the financial flow into your life, seek out the evidence that supports beliefs of abundance. The Universe will always support your dreams!

6th April
Ask for Help

Do you ask for what you want? Really? Sometimes we think we are asking for what we want but it is more of a well-disguised hint that relies on the other person's mind-reading skills. Too often you can hear people tell someone what they want from a friend or partner or child but fail to ask the person involved directly. That simply doesn't make a recipe for happy and inspired relationships. Today is the day to really identify what you want and then to ask for help and support from the people around you in a clear and compelling way. Help them to understand not just how it will benefit you but the reciprocal benefits for them—which could just be that they have a happier friend, colleague or lover! Of course, the flip side of that is that everyone is equally entitled to refuse our request. And when that happens, the best solution is to just find ways to give it to yourself. When we meet our own needs, we get to experience joy both ways—the pleasure of giving and the delight of receiving.

7th April
Nudges

When we have a longing or desire for things to change, the Universe is always aware of what we want. Sometimes we get to move in the direction of our dreams gently but sometimes (especially when it is something we have wanted for a while or with great intensity), the next step comes as an almighty shove. In other words, the Universe decides to shake it all up! If we perceive these disturbances as being a major issue and become fixated on problem solving or trying to minimise the damage, we tend to find ourselves wading treacle. But if we can stay detached enough to move with the Universal push, we can find ourselves propelled along a new and exciting path. Things can happen very quickly when we are prepared to take a leap of faith!

8th April
Todoitis

If you ever get the feeling that your life is being overrun by the amount of tasks or activities you have to do, then you probably have a bout of *todoitis*. Whenever we feel obligated to do things for ourselves or other people, our get-to-dos have turned into got-to-dos! The antidote to this is simple—restore choice! When we are at choice, we always get to experience freedom to live the lives we want and those annoying obligations disappear. There are always alternatives in any situation. So today seek alternatives for those got-to-dos. You may still do the original action but now you will feel greater peace and freedom because it is a choice not an obligation.

9th April
Gentleness

Today the JoyScope invites you to be gentle. Gentleness is hugely under-rated. When we are kind and loving towards our self and others, we lower our resistance and bring ourselves into alignment with life. When you catch yourself working hard to make things happen, stop trying to push the river and instead find ways to go with the flow. You may need to take a step back from your current circumstances and challenges, and put your attention on your inner world of thoughts, feelings and emotions. Rather than trying to resolve situations through forcing action, find inspiration through reflection, contemplation and meditation. Tread gently through your life and allow peace and tranquility to flood in.

༺✦༻

10th April
Cut Out the Middleman

Would you like more love in your life? Today the message is a reminder that love begins at home! So if you would like to experience more love, cut out the middleman and give it to yourself. Love your grey hair, your balding patch or your bumpy bits! Love yourself when you are grumpy, grouchy or out of sorts. Love yourself when you have made a mistake or put your foot in it. Love yourself when you have said something you didn't mean or forgot to say something that really mattered. Love yourself when you feel sad or vulnerable or afraid. Love yourself no matter what has happened or will happen. When we are more loving towards ourselves as well as others, we invite more love into our lives. So go on, love yourself freely today.

༺✦༻

11th April
Delegation

Inside all of us there is an inner manager. This is the aspect of us that we can delegate roles to. We can give our manager jobs to complete that don't require our continual conscious intervention. There are many different life tasks that we could turn over to our manager but it does require us getting out of our own way. Perhaps you have a decision to make, need a solution to a problem or want a new idea or inspiration. If so, delegate it to your inner manager. Let them take on the task, wait for them to report back and trust that they will handle it perfectly. Your inner manager can be your most valuable asset. Give him or her the opportunity to demonstrate their worth today!

12th April
Time Thieves

For people who have busy lives, one of their greatest desires is to have more time. But time is a finite resource and no matter how hard we wish, there will always be 60 seconds in a minute, 60 minutes in an hour and 24 hours in a day. However, we can increase our energy and that leads to an overall sense of having more space in our lives and a feeling of being able to achieve more. Today is a good day to spot the energy drains in your life. Sometimes these are the littlest things that mildly irritate or frustrate us but because they are so small, we do nothing about it and they continue to drain our energy away. Pick one thing to rectify today. It could be a minor repair job in the home, a call that you have been putting off or some clutter clearing. Free up some energy and notice the benefits in your life.

13th April
Spontaneity

Have you noticed how some of the best experiences happen when you least expect it? Would you like to have more of them? It can be easier than we think. Good times happen when our resistance towards life is low. That is why these experiences seem to happen spontaneously when our attention is elsewhere or we are distracted from any issues going on in our lives. It is therefore not about lowering our expectations so much as not expecting any experience to be different to how it is. When we just hold the belief that we live in a co-operative universe and that life will work out well, we can allow each and every event to unfold in the best way possible and we just get to enjoy the ride...spontaneously!

14th April
Distractions

In this era, there is always something to occupy our time. Numerous distractions can take over our lives. Long to-do lists of things that we *should* be doing weigh heavily. Information overloads us from the TV, internet, newspapers and so on, most of which is less than inspiring. So there is real value in taking time out (whether that is an hour, a day, or even a year) to create space. In that stillness, you can make a decision to become selective about where you spend your time. Choose wisely what to give your attention to. Create more opportunities in your life to be uplifted and feel good. It could be making a decision to turn off that soap on TV and pick an inspiring movie or comedy to watch instead. It could be a refreshing and rejuvenating walk in nature rather than heading straight for the sofa. It could be a pamper day at a spa rather than the hustle and bustle of a Saturday afternoon shopping in town. There are countless options and only you can know what is right for you. The challenge is simply to make it a conscious and deliberate choice rather than an ongoing habit.

15th April
Love Your Fear Gremlins

You are probably familiar with the phrase *"Feel the fear and do it anyway"** but what about *"Feel the love and do it anyway!"* When we are facing a challenge or even reaching for our dreams, fear gremlins can pop up and try to dissuade us from moving forwards. If we attempt to ignore or crush those little voices, they only become amplified. But if we can feel appreciation for their service and offer our love and respect, we can reassure the part of us that is fearful and reassign it to the task of supporting us instead. So, if you have a fear gremlin, ask yourself how it is serving you. Does it want to keep you safe or protect you from disappointment or the negative judgments of others? Thank the gremlin for caring enough to speak up, create a compelling vision of why it is important to you, and notice how quickly the voice of fear becomes the voice of love.

*Susan Jeffers used this expression when she wrote her book "Feel The Fear And Do It Anyway" which is well worth reading!

16th April
In the Moment

Have you noticed that when you are completely in the moment, engrossed in the bliss of what is happening around you and totally enjoying yourself that all those niggles and problems seem to miraculously disappear? The JoyScope message for today is to find something that absorbs your attention and allows you to focus on being in *now*. It could be a meditative practice, taking a walk in nature, playing sport, gardening, cooking a meal or anything else that draws you in. As you bring your awareness back to the present, notice how everything else in your life takes on a new perspective. So what was that thing that *used* to bother you?

17th April
Unconditional Love

Unconditional love has nothing to do with anyone else; it is a state of being that resides completely within us. When we love with expectations that another person should behave a certain way, we simply set ourselves up for failure. No one will be able to please us all of the time and as soon as they act in a way that doesn't match our requirements, the love will cease to flow. Yet when we are not being loving, we hurt ourselves the most. So today the message from the JoyScope is to keep the centre of your love firmly within. Love not because someone is doing things in a certain way. Love because you are a loving being. It's who you *really* are!

18th April
Bugbears

We all have our little bugbears in life. Whether it is sorting finances, paying bills or managing paperwork or those less than inspiring household chores such as cleaning, washing, ironing and so on, or perhaps those irritating family members and work colleagues who just have a knack of pushing the right buttons at the wrong time! These can cause immense frustration, impatience and even stress— if we let them. The only reason that something can irritate us is when we are not allowing ourselves to see the fuller picture. When we tap into what it means to have a clean house, organised administration, a family and a job, we find that those issues seem far less significant. It's corny but true that many of these frustrations are bi-products of our success. If we didn't have a house or family or job or money, our circumstances and challenges would be very different! So the next time an irritant shows up in your life, thank the cause and take the hit of reminding yourself how successful and blessed you are.

19th April
Common Ground

All conflict is the result of disagreements, often minor when they begin, that get magnified over time as we give our attention to them. Conflict and disharmony depletes our energy reserves and affects our alignment. When we search for and focus on the common ground, we come back into alignment, not just with the other person but also much more importantly within ourselves. Simply put, we don't feel good when we are disagreeing with others, so it is ourselves we affect the most! If you find yourself in a disagreement today, just pause and ask yourself what is the joint experience you are having and how do you want it to be instead. As soon as you do that, you may just be surprised at how quickly you find agreement.

20th April
Capability

Most of us have been conditioned into thinking that our ability to achieve our dreams is directly related to our skills and ability. Yet this is only a fraction of the story. We all know of people who have been hugely successful, seemingly out of nothing, whilst there are other people who never seem to realise their true potential. Our belief and expectation have far more impact on what we can or cannot do. We can do extraordinary things when our belief in our capability is unwavering. So today believe that what you want is possible. Believe that it is inevitable. You have the capability to manifest all of your dreams and desires.

21st April
Journaling

In our fast-paced world driven by technology and the need for speed, journaling has become a lost art form. The process of journaling opens the flow of communication between your present awareness and your higher consciousness. It is not about dutifully recording all of your experiences but more a way of encouraging inner dialogue and self-reflection. There are so many options—you can make it a daily practice as a gift of me-time or you can write on an ad-hoc basis when your mood moves you. You can journal in story form or just use bullets to capture the salient points of an experience. You can create a computer file or buy a beautifully bound notebook. Journaling is a private practice. Simply do what feels best for you. As you commit to this process, you will uncover the wisdom of your soul.

22nd April
Diversity

The world is a beautiful and eclectic blend of different people with different personalities and different habits. That is what makes it such a rich and stimulating planet. Imagine if we were all exactly the same—acting the same, talking the same, thinking the same! How quickly would boredom set in if you were experiencing Groundhog Day in every conversation? Yet isn't it easy to forget this appreciation of variety in the moment that someone's behaviour is irritating or frustrating to us? Don't we start wishing that person would just be a little more like us? But they can only be who they are and it isn't their job to please us, it is their job to please themselves. So today, notice the times when you start wishing that someone would be different, then stop and pause and remember that the real beauty lies in diversity!

23rd April
Stop and Be

Today is an excellent day for just stopping and simply being! Whether you choose to take a whole day for pottering and moodling or whether it is just carving out a slice of precious time to do absolutely nothing. No TV or radio or telephone calls. No pondering the past or contemplating the future. No list-making or note-taking. Just being at one with the magnificence of who you are. Perfect, whole and complete, just as you are. When we create quality time to connect with our inner selves, we foster our inner relationship. We strengthen our convictions, tap into our dreams and desires and create an abundance of good feelings like peace, confidence, love and bliss. Now is that something worth stopping for?

24th April
Best Friend

The message from the JoyScope today is to be your own best friend. We are often much kinder and more loving to our friends than we are to ourselves. We respond to our friends' needs with generosity and patience yet we can be harsh and critical when we are in need. When things don't go to plan, do you criticize and blame yourself or are you supportive and reassuring? If you catch yourself having a low moment today, be gentle with yourself. Self-soothe any negative thoughts or inner dialogue. Treat yourself as you would a best friend. When we treat ourselves with the love and respect we deserve, we give others the permission to do the same. Self-love is the beginning of a wonderful, life-long relationship.

25th April
Prioritisation

Today the JoyScope invites you to consider your priorities. When we have long to-do lists, it is a little too easy to get so wrapped up in urgency that we forget to take care of the foundational necessities. We may skip meals, deprive ourselves of sleep or cancel the gym membership. It can seem as though we are handling things when we are ticking tasks off our action lists but when we are neglecting our own needs, our energy tank rapidly runs low! If you are juggling multiple commitments, ensure that you also build in time to top up your tank. Self-care is the cornerstone to a happy, fulfilling and vibrant life.

26th April
Wants and Needs

Have you noticed how children are inclined to use the words *want* and *need* interchangeably? Are we really that different? What we need is fairly simple and basic. We *need* food, water, shelter from the elements and sleep in order to survive. Yet do we really need much more than that? When we turn our wants into needs, we create a form of dependency and attachment. It also continues to focus our attention on the absence of having it. For example, "*I need more money*" lines you up with more scarcity whereas "*I want more money*" changes it to the desire for abundance. Today, even if you are not stating it out loud, just be aware of where you have unconsciously created needs. Turn them back to wants and notice how much energy it frees up.

27th April
Extra Time

Queuing and waiting is part of life. So what do you do with all of that *wasted time* when your appointment is delayed, you find yourself in a shop or traffic queue or someone is late to your meeting? In fact, it isn't the time that is wasted. The clock keeps ticking in exactly the same way regardless of how we are spending the seconds, minutes and hours. But as soon as we slip into irritation, complaining or arguing with the reality of the situation, then we give away our time to negativity, and that is the real waste. Instead, it is worth having your personal toolkit to allow you to make the most of every circumstance. Carry a book or Kindle and delayed appointments and meetings become extra relaxation or learning time. Audio books and CDs turn traffic jams into story time. Even shopping queues are a great opportunity to practice visualisation and meditation—don't worry if you nod off as the person behind you will always let you know when it is your turn! When you practice playing with wasted time, you may just find that instead of feeling frustrated, you start to look forward to those moments and wishing for more.

28th April
Guides

Many spiritual and metaphysical works teach that we all have guides, our unseen friends and helpers gently supporting us on our paths. They report that these come in different guises including angels, archetypes and family/friends who have passed on. Maybe you believe in this concept or maybe you don't. But a fun game to play is to imagine if you did have a guide, what form they might take. If you could pick, what guide would you like to have supporting you on your journey? Would it be a fairy or an elf for fun and playfulness? A soldier or a warrior for strength and courage? A guru or spiritual sage for wisdom and insight? Or maybe a merlin or witch for magic and miracles. The choice is yours—and you never know, you may actually be tapping into a higher energy in the process.

29th April
Resourcefulness

Sometimes we are faced with challenges or issues that test our resourcefulness. But remember that even in moments when we are living what we *don't want*, there is still value in the experience. Resourcefulness isn't about having an easy life – it is the ability to use our inner strengths and qualities to respond positively to whatever happens. In fact, those times that test you most provide the opportunities to really discover the depths of your talents. So today the JoyScope invites you to reflect on your life to date. Where have you demonstrated resourcefulness? What did you learn about yourself? Write a list of the qualities you discovered lying deep inside you? And as you consider that list perhaps you can almost be eagerly anticipating the next test of your ability to discover even more.

30th April
L.A.D

Today the JoyScope invites you to get present to your life. Far too many of us are suffering from LAD (Life Awareness Deficiency). Our focus is consistently pulled towards all of the distractions and diversions and our experience of life therefore becomes diluted and dispersed. Being fully present allows you to fully engage in everything that happens. This not only means being in the now rather than the past or future but also to be deeply aware of your inner world of emotions too. When you give your focused attention to that, life becomes more authentic and inspired. So today, as you go about your day, take time not just to notice what is happening but also to ask yourself how you feel. You can even set a regular reminder (for example, an alarm on your watch or phone) to encourage this process. As you condition the process of checking in, you tune in much more easily to the richness of every experience.

1st May
Meaning-Making

Life is just a series of events and experiences but, as human beings, we are meaning-making machines and so we have emotional responses to what is happening. We don't always get to (consciously) choose our experiences but we do get to choose the meaning we apply to it. So what if you could just change the meaning you are assigning to your experience? Well the good news is that you always get to choose the story you are telling yourself. So if you want a different emotional journey, change your stories! Today, if you find yourself feeling challenged, look for a positive slant on the experience and notice how much better it feels. Choose to find the reasons and meanings that inspire, uplift and delight you and it really will be a great day.

2nd May
Switching Views

Ever heard the expression, *"A change is as good as a rest"*? One of the benefits of getting a change of scene is that it brings a different point of view on your life. When we take a break, we are able to come back to our current situation with fresh eyes and see things that perhaps we were missing. So, today, make a commitment to find a new perspective. It could be booking a holiday or a weekend away, taking a day trip or simply finding a different route to work. When we expand our perceptions, we open our mind to new concepts. Stretch beyond the familiar and discover what else is really possible for you.

3rd May
Flowing with the River

The art of true happiness is the ability to allow the natural flow of life. Our resistance to what is happening causes all of our suffering and confusion. When we live in harmony with the way things are, we release the resistance and reconnect to a state of well-being and happiness. So instead of paddling frantically to where you think you want to be, let go of the oars and let the river take you downstream. The river of life will twist and turn but the ride is much smoother when you go with the flow.

4th May
Standards

In this fast-paced world, it can seem to be more important to get something done than to do it to a certain standard. It's not that there is anything wrong with taking short-cuts but if the completion of the task becomes more important than the process of doing it, we often take all of the enjoyment out of it and set ourselves up for feeling like hamsters on a wheel (going round and round without getting anywhere)! What happens when we slow down and totally immerse ourselves in what we are doing? Even the most mundane jobs can become fascinating—washing-up becomes a light display of bubbles, filing brings a sense of peace and organisation to the mind, cutting the grass can be an opportunity to connect with the earth. Take time today and hold yourself to the highest standards in everything that you do and notice how your experiences change. The bi-product is that you might just find you get more done than you think is possible.

5th May
Body Talk

Today is a great day to tune into your body. We are bombarded with picture perfect models in magazines and other media that have often been airbrushed beyond recognition. If you go to the gym, you may be surrounded by people who are punishing their bodies into submission. Bulging muscles aren't always a sign of health and vitality when weight training is done at the expense of a general fitness routine. It's not to say that we shouldn't keep ourselves in good shape but that is about being fit for life not trying to measure up to a cultural ideal that most of us are not physically designed to be. Today support your body from the inside out. Tune into what it needs most to encourage vitality and well-being. It may be some high intensity training but it is just as likely to be a gentle stroll or swim. When we ask our bodies what they most need, the answers are sometimes surprising. What does your body choose today?

6th May
Laughter

Life is supposed to be fun! Ever had times when you laughed so hard that your sides hurt and tears rolled down your face? The message from the JoyScope today is to seek out sidesplitting fun and laughter. It could be renting a comedy film, going to a comedy club or just meeting up with a good friend and reminiscing about some of those funny things that have happened in your life. When we laugh, we pump feel-good endorphins through our bodies, which has a positive impact on our whole well-being. And the other side effect is that laughter is catching. As you ridiculously enjoy yourself, notice the fun that happens around you. So smile, giggle and chuckle your way through today!

7th May
Release the Guilt

Did you know you are the most important person in *your* world? Whenever we make a decision that is authentically right for us, it has to be right for other people—they just might not be able to appreciate it yet. We came here to live our lives our way. We may choose to notice and learn from the best of others but that comes from choice not obligation. Guilt will always prevent you from experiencing alignment in your life and moving forwards in the direction you want. So, today, release yourself from duty and obligation and feel the freedom of being all of who you really are. Take this as a sign that it is okay for you to do that thing you want to do.

8th May
Inspiration

I - It's
N - not
S - seeking
P - perfection:
I - it's
R - recognising
A - all
T - the
I - insights
O - occurring
N - now!

9th May
Productivity

One of the greatest issues of our lifetime will be managing our productivity. Demands on our time and energy have never been higher both personally and professionally. The question of our era seems to be *"How can I get more done in less time*?" Do you ever find yourself under pressure to get things done only to find that your productivity seems to dip at the most inconvenient times? Well it may not be a coincidence. When demands on us are high, we are more likely to be pulled out of our natural flow and spend too much time over-thinking and trying to work things out. But the solution for everything already exists so instead of pushing on, we often become more productive when we stop and allow the right things to find us. Why not slow down and notice how things change around you when you do? Slowing down may well be the most productive thing you can do.

10th May
Choice Points

Do you ever find yourself struggling to make a decision? In these times of uncertainty, it can be less easy to predict how things will turn out. But there is a simpler way to handle choice points. Your emotions will give you guidance on the next step to take. If it feels good or feels like relief then you are lining up with your dreams. If it feels heavy or complicated, you are probably heading in the wrong direction! Learning to trust our inner guidance is key to making good decisions. Yes, you want to ensure that you gather enough information to understand the situation first—sometimes indecision is just trying to reach a conclusion before you have the right amount of data. But after that, your feelings will guide you all the way. When it is the right path, it may feel natural or exciting or inspiring. It may even seem a little big and overwhelming but the over-riding sense inside will be good. And the best news is that often, it doesn't really matter what we pick. It will always work out well so long as, once we have decided, we line up with the choice and focus on the rewards we want to reap.

11th May
Beyond Revenge

If we perceive that have been wronged in some way, it is completely understandable to feel like we need to take revenge. It may not be as dramatic as trying to intentionally cause hurt or damage but may be in a more subtle way such as saying harsh words, creating complications, being uncooperative or even withdrawing our love and attention. But the truth is that whilst it is natural to feel vengeful and it is good to acknowledge and honour our feelings, when we take action from that emotional state, the person we hurt most is always ourselves. We are meant to be loving and when we are anything less than that, we deprive ourselves of our natural birthright and hold happiness at arms-length. The most powerful form of revenge is to use our feelings towards creating more good in our lives and the lives of others. In the short-term lashing out may feel validating but any time we rise above a situation and take the higher ground, we create bucket-loads of self-esteem and confidence in the longer term. So next time you feel hurt, what will you choose?

12th May
Wellness

Our natural birthright is to be well. All illness—whether a cold or something more serious—is just a blip in the body's system. When we notice that there is *dis-ease*, we are being encouraged to give ourselves a health check and to nourish and nurture our way back to total and complete health. It can be less than easy to focus on well-being when our bodies (and, in some cases, Doctors) are presenting evidence to the contrary but there are countless examples of people self-healing from even the most serious and bleak of prognoses. Being well is always an inside job. Our job is to allow it. How we do that will always be unique to us—we just need to follow our hearts and do the things that *feel* healthy. That could be eating certain foods, taking exercise, surrounding ourselves with positive and life-affirming friends and resting and rejuvenating. Be easy and light about what you choose to do. Our bodies appreciate gentleness. Your body knows how to be well.

13th May
Segmenting

When we live busy lives, we can often feel like we are spreading ourselves thinly across multiple demands. Whether that is work pressures, family commitments, or other projects and obligations. Do you ever find yourself needing to focus at work but feeling distracted by other things going on in your life? Or wanting to spend quality time with the family but unable to drag yourself mentally away from work? The easiest way to create boundaries between commitments is to *segment* your time. Wherever you are and whatever you are doing, practice giving that your full undivided attention. Mentally *park* everything else until the appropriate time. The quality of your experiences and your relationships will dramatically improve when you are able to be fully present to what (or who) is going on around you.

14th May
Regression

Sometimes we can find ourselves acting out of character. Even the smallest things seem to be able to take us into the most unresourceful states. We might get angry or upset or annoyed or sad—often knowing in the moment that our reaction is disproportional to the experience we are having, yet unable to stop ourselves. How can that happen? When we are young, we don't have the same capacity for understanding circumstances and experiences. In response to childhood fear or trauma, a part of us gets stuck in that memory so that when a similar situation occurs later in life, we regress right back to our younger selves. As we do so, we literally take on being that age again. So if we were six when we first had those feelings, we take on the persona of a six-year-old and unfortunately, we now only have access to what we knew when we were six. No wonder we feel so unresourceful! The good news is that we can learn to self-heal. When you next find yourself regressing, just remind yourself of all of the wonderful learnings, qualities and strengths you have now. What do you now have or know that would transform the situation? As you tap into all of who you are, you realise that what was once real can no longer hold you back. You reconnect fully to all of your magnificence once more.

15th May
Responsiveness

One of the key skills in life is being able to decide when to take action and when not to. The challenge is that in order to make this decision we have to be aware that there is one. Often we are already triggered into our response before we have fully considered our options. We have reacted automatically and unconsciously. So it is time to develop our awareness. Before you begin to respond to any challenge, it is a valuable exercise to take a deep breath and consider alternatives. Do you want to change your circumstances from a place of powerlessness? Are you hoping to make someone change his or her ways? Are you feeling defensive or angry? In these situations, it is likely that any action you take will cause more harm than good. Instead of trying to force change on the outside world, find ways to create shifts on the inside. You could choose to turn a blind eye or alter your viewpoint or just choose a different response. When you make your reaction a conscious decision, you master responsiveness.

16th May
Charity

Here in the UK a wonderful phenomenon has emerged. At periodic intervals, national charitable events take place that raise huge amounts of money for extremely worthy causes. It is nothing short of a miracle that millions of pounds can be donated in a matter of hours. People don red noses or run in fancy dress costumes or sit in baths of beans in the name of charity. A wonderful sense of fun and community is fostered. What is more interesting is that we generally wait for these dates to happen to enter into the spirit of contribution. But why wait? Doesn't it feel good to be collaborating, co-operating and giving back? So why not make a decision today to give generously of your time and love. You not only get to be an uplifter in other people's lives, but you raise your own vibe too.

17th May
Limitless Potential

Within every one of us exists limitless potential. Often we do not know what we are capable of until a situation tests our abilities. Like the famous story of the grandmother who lifted a car to free her trapped grandson, sometimes our potential only becomes apparent when we are challenged to the extreme. So the message from the JoyScope today is to examine your own capability *before* the challenge occurs! What do you dream of that you have not yet fulfilled? What secret talents do you harbour that you have not yet expressed? Your potential is your own unique contribution to the world. You don't need to wait to share the best of you with the world. Begin today!

18th May
Inner Truths

Today the JoyScope invites you to find your inner truths. When we are tuned into them, our truths guide us on our journey but when we are not connected, we can find that we start to feel off track. Your truths are completely unique to you. They consist of your values, your dreams, your understandings and all that you have learnt—and no one else will know what you know to be true. But there is a cautionary note. Our truths are often masked by the ego's needs for safety, control and perfection. Any time that we find that we are unquestionably conforming to cultural, social or family expectations, we have lost sight of our own truth.

So how do we know the difference between an inner truth and an external obligation? Because of the way we feel. A truth is a deep and unwavering knowing that puts fire and passion in your belly. On the other hand, a rule will feel heavier and repressive and tends to be located in or around your head. You may even experience it as a voice from a parent or authority figure. When you notice you aren't tapping into your inner guidance, simply pull all of your attention to your heart and naval area and drop into your knowing. The answer will come when you ask what is true for you.

19th May
Still Voice Within

In the hustle and bustle of life, it's not always easy to create time for stillness. When we are busy getting things done, we don't always give our subconscious mind the opportunity to offer guidance. However, when we take time out to just sit and be, we allow that communication to come through. We can listen to that quiet voice within that guides us in the direction we want to go. So the message from the JoyScope is to pay close attention to the whispers from your soul. Underneath the chatterbox is a powerful, supportive voice that offers infinite wisdom for living an inspired life. You may find you are gently nudged towards a specific action. If so, take note and something wonderful is sure to happen.

20th May
Turn It Off

Are you an over-thinker? Having a powerful computer between our ears is both a blessing and a curse. It allows us to plan ahead and develop ideas which can enhance the quality of our life, yet when it is always switched on, it can be a real challenge to stop thinking and be in the moment, enjoying our experiences. So does your computer need time to rest? Can you flick the switch and set it to standby mode? All computers need a break (and sometimes a full re-boot!) and our minds are no exception. So the message today is to take time out from thinking, planning and analysing. Focus instead on the small things that enrich our lives—the beauty of petals on a flower, a smile on the face of a child, the warmth of a hot bath, the taste of our favourite food or the rhythm of a certain music track. The choice is yours. Your mind will enjoy the rest!

21st May
Positivity Seeking

Life can be many things—fun, exciting, inspiring and passionate or tiring, mundane, conflict-ridden and frustrating. The truth is that we get to choose. We can make it an exhausting struggle or we can make it a blissful journey because it is always down to us. Yes, people may do those things that annoy you. Yes, sometimes you might not get exactly what you think you want. Yes, there will be blips and bumps along the way. But if you take time to focus on the good stuff, no matter how small and insignificant it seems, you may just find that even in the most challenging of times there is always more to appreciate than to bemoan. Become a positivity seeker. Make it into a game with yourself to be searching for the hidden uplifting gem in every situation. Sometimes the most fun you can have is simply to be happy for no reason at all.

22nd May
Melt-ups

Sometimes we can be merrily traveling along our path when our world crashes in and we find ourselves in meltdown! Anyone who has experienced a meltdown knows how intense the emotional response can be—we can find ourselves totally demoralised or even paralysed by uncertainty. Although our initial reaction can be genuine and authentic, we often exacerbate the problem when we form opinions on how well we are handling our meltdown. It's those feelings about our feelings that trip us up and keep us stuck. Thinking we should have known better is never helpful. Aren't we always doing the best that we can in every situation? Why would you want to beat up on yourself for that? In fact, when we allow ourselves to experience a meltdown without judgment, what we often discover is that it was only ever really a melt-up! Something needed to change in order for the next part of your journey to reveal itself. So next time it all appears to be going belly-up, embrace your melt-up and be excited about what is around the next corner.

23rd May
Problem-Solving

Albert Einstein famously said that problems couldn't be solved by the same level of thinking that created them. If we want to make a change, we need to shift our thinking. There are always a number of different courses of action available but if we are still locked into focusing on the issue, we won't be able to access these alternatives. So if you are facing a challenge and want an inspired solution, the first step in the process is to shift your state. Make peace with the current situation, turn your attention to aspects of your life that are working or just feel a little better than the problem. As your raise your vibe, limitless possibilities will begin to emerge and then the only difficulty you will face is which great option to pick.

24th May
Feeling Good Now!

Do you ever have the feeling that it is going to be a really good day? If your response is yes, then you know that when you have that feeling you are probably going to be right. So would you like to have that feeling every day? The fastest way to create that feeling is to either focus on one of those *best* days from the past or the positive anticipation of a good day that you know is on its way. Our subconscious doesn't recognise the difference between remembered or future events, so when we access positive thoughts, the good feelings flow immediately. Try it now and feel instantly great!

25th May
Finding Your Purpose

What's your life purpose? That question seems to appear at different points throughout our lives. It can leave us feeling inspired and encouraged or uncertain and unsure but it does provide an opportunity for us to review and reflect on our lives. Are we heading in the direction that we want? Do we have the passion and enthusiasm to live a great life? Are we in-tune with our inner guidance? We can make finding our purpose a fun game. We can simply engage in the process of self-discovery and be astounded by the way that things unfold. Of course the truth is that our real purpose is to live fully, openly and joyfully—and everything else is simply a bonus.

26th May
Faith

Today the message from the JoyScope is to have faith. There are times that no matter how great our desire and how aligned we feel about getting what we want, it still seems not to happen. This is where faith comes in. Universal energy is conspiring to support the manifestation of your dreams but it will *always* choose the best means of delivery! Sometimes what we think we want (that relationship, that job, that opportunity) is not in our highest and best interests. When we remember there is an endless supply of opportunities coming our way, we can turn it over to the Universe to decide when and where it should happen. Trust and have faith. It is all happening perfectly!

27th May
Check-in (2)

As we approach the middle of the year, it is worth taking time out to reflect on how your year is going. Maybe it has been a wonderful six months, maybe it has been less than great. But rather than judging your success (or lack of it), the JoyScope just invites you to become the witness, gently observing the events of the year so far. As you simply notice and acknowledge your experiences, consider what you would like to happen for the second half of this year. What would need to be true on New Year's Eve for you to celebrate unreservedly! Set your intentions now. Know whatever you want can happen and you can never get it wrong. The Universe will move to support your dreams.

28th May
Life Rituals

Today the JoyScope would like to invite you to explore the idea of life rituals. Whilst visualising what we want is a large part of the creation process, we also need to be in alignment with our dreams and desires and that is where rituals and practice can be extremely beneficial. So, today, choose an area of your life that you would like to enhance. It could be health and well-being, relationships, career or family. What is one daily practice that you could introduce that would support your dream? For example, if you want boundless energy and vitality, you may commit to eating more organic and natural food. Or if you want a stronger relationship, you may commit to communicating openly with your partner each day. Have a play with some different daily rituals and you may be delightfully surprised with how aligning they are.

29th May
Getting it done!

Have you ever wished for a few more hours in a day or a couple more days in a week just to get everything done? When we are busy with personal or professional projects, it's so easy to fall into despondent thinking and to worry that we will never get it all done in time. But somehow, we do manage to find a way to pull it out of the bag, no matter how last minute it may seem. We might have to find a few shortcuts or it may not be everything we had imagined, but when the time arrives, we often find it is all as it is meant to be. So what if we just cut out the middle phase of worry and anxiety and went straight from feeling excited about the idea to the satisfaction of completion? Would it make any difference to the project? Maybe not. Would it make any difference to us? Most definitely! And of course, when we are feeling good, we might just get more done.

30th May
Perspective Shifts

There are always different ways of viewing the world. Do you relish the *details* in a situation? Or are you more of a *big picture* thinker? Both views are equally valid but we will tend to have a preference (and more natural ability) for one of them. And there is great value in each approach; the key is to know when to use them in the best way. Big picture views are great for creative insights and a sense of purpose. Taking the helicopter perspective on your life can help you to understand the direction you are going in and how everything links together. Detailed views are great for planning and organising. When you are feeling good about what you are doing, tuning in can help you to bask in all the wonderful aspects of a situation. You can focus upon all the specifics—where you are, how you feel, what you see and hear, who is with you and milk every moment. But if what you are focusing on doesn't feel so good, it is best to take a step back, regain a big picture view, and get a whole new perspective on things. The invitation from the JoyScope today is to play with switching views. Have fun discovering which approach feels better for you today.

31st May
Overcoming Challenges

Whenever we face a challenge in life, we have a choice as to how we handle it. One way is to focus on the problem and allow ourselves to become overwhelmed or fearful about what might happen. The other way is to use every issue as an opportunity to raise our game. When we stay focused on the outcome that we really want, all blocks are only temporary and they will provide learning and feedback for how we can make adjustments to our own alignment. If you are facing challenges today, choose the path of least resistance. Accept what is and allow the creative insights and ideas to flow. The solution may be better than you could possibly imagine.

1st June
Distortion

When we look at the stars shining in the sky, we don't always appreciate their size and the power they hold. Distance distorts our perception of what we see. The same is true in life. Sometimes the things that seem big are really tiny in terms of their significance. And the things that seem smallest actually really matter most. So the message from the JoyScope today is to check your perspective. Are you giving most of your attention to the things that are really most important to you? Problems and niggles will come and go but the most valuable aspects of life will always remain.

2nd June
Mistakes

Are you willing to make mistakes? Our automatic response might be yes, but really consider how willing you are to get something wrong. Most of us have a natural risk-avoidance driver, especially when it comes to the important things in life.

The thought of taking a wrong turn or falling flat on our face is anything but appealing. But sometimes our best learning comes from trying something new and being willing to make it up as you go along. Of course that means that you have to let go of the need to be perfect! But perfection is vastly over-rated. The real thrill of life comes from discovering a different way, finding what works and what doesn't and being on the leading edge of something new. Embrace and celebrate each and every one of your mistakes and watch as the path to success unfolds in front of you.

3rd June
Believe in Miracles

There is nothing that cannot happen today! Can you find the truth in that declaration? Every day brings with it an infinite number of opportunities. The only thing that ever holds us back is our expectation about what can happen. Perhaps you can recall a time when something so unexpected and wonderful happened that it felt like a miracle. Maybe you know others who seem to experience miracles on a regular basis. Today believe in miracles. Open your heart and mind to the idea that something amazing could happen and you may just get to be very pleasantly surprised. A miracle could be just around the corner!

4th June
Love Versus Fear

There are really only two ways to respond to any situation in life—one is a fear-based response, the other is to respond in a loving way. We can decide that the Universe is against us or we can remember that the Universe always loves us unconditionally. That doesn't necessarily mean that you need to love a situation (or person) that is causing you pain but it is about loving the *you* that is having the experience. Every event is an opportunity to learn and grow. It is always more comfortable to grow through joyful experiences than through struggle, but when we are willing to embrace the learning the situation will seem to miraculously resolve. So, today, whatever you are experiencing, be gentle with yourself and love yourself into your personal expansion.

5th June
Own Goals

Having goals is great as it focuses the mind and spirit and can motivate you to take action. But when we set a target out in the future, we often only reward ourselves when we have achieved it. When we set the goal it is easy to get going because we are tuned into how it will feel to arrive at the goal destination—our end state. But if it is a big and audacious goal, it may be sometime before we start to see the results we want. Many goals fail because we lose the connection to our end state when the results are slow. Goals are much more effective when you remind yourself of the end state every step of the way. It keeps you focused and inspired on your way to what you want. And, of course, the best part of any goal is being able to feel wonderful along the way.

6th June
Love Vitamins

There is no better antidote to any issue or problem in our life than a good dose of love! If you are facing a challenge right now or even if things are going swimmingly well and you just want to raise your vibe, prescribing yourself all the good emotions associated with being loving and loved are a sure fire way of feeling instantly better. So what vitamins do you need to take—a spoonful of self-love or unconditional love or maybe the mother of all vitamins, universal love? Take one (or more) as often as you want. The only downside to overdosing on love is that it can be rather infectious to those around you! So if you do accidentally take one too many love vitamins, I wonder what magic could happen today?

7th June
Past Definitions

How does your past define who you are today? Do you look back and reflect on your journey with pride and appreciation or do aspects of the past still cause you to feel hurt or wronged in some way. One is a recipe for ultimate success, the other is a sure-fire way to feel bitter and hold you back from living an inspired life. There is not one person who has lived a significant proportion of their life without experiencing immense challenges. Ask anyone about their biggest challenge and you will hear stories of overcoming seemingly insurmountable adversities. But these can be the moments when we discover the depths of our resourcefulness and what we are truly capable of. When we trust that it is all working out perfectly, we can allow these challenges to become a springboard for taking our lives to the next level. What we learn through the experience can become a reason to celebrate as we allow ourselves to grow emotionally and spiritually. Rise above those difficulties and show the world the truth of the person you have become.

8th June
Multi-tasking

There is a great deal of pressure on us these days to become masters of multi-tasking. Demands on our time and resources have never been higher so we often find ourselves juggling multiple activities at the same time. Even just something simple like eating lunch whilst responding to emails has a significant impact on our lives. When we are splitting our attention on many different things, our minds and bodies never get the quality of experience that we really deserve. For example, you cannot be fully present with your children and try to do work/housework at the same time. There will always be times where there is little choice but it is worth noting when this has become habitual. So the message today is to find opportunities to give your full, undivided attention to just one thing. There is great power in presence!

9th June
Inspiring Love

An inspired relationship is based on unconditional love. Love isn't about liking the same things, being in agreement or even approving of their behaviour but it is a willingness to allow our partner to be their authentic self. We are on our own unique paths and although we may choose to share the journey, our ultimate destination is ours and ours alone. We can never know what is right for another person. We can only trust and have faith that they are finding their own way. When we have the courage to stand back, to view them (and their choices) through the eyes of love, and to let things naturally unfold, we strengthen our bond and an inspired relationship is the gift we give ourselves.

10th June
Celebrate

Today the JoyScope is encouraging you to find reasons to celebrate. The world is moving so fast that we are often on to the next thing before we have really acknowledged what we have achieved. When we acknowledge life, we send a message of affirmation to the Universe saying "*I did this*" and it creates more opportunities for you to celebrate. You get to decide what is worth celebrating —from the big successes to the smallest of achievements—they are all a great excuse to get your party shoes on. Life is short so milk the moment and find out how much fun you can have with a life of celebration.

11th June
Life-steps

Life happens incrementally. If we want to manifest our wishes and desires, we only need to take it step-by-step. If we have a big and exciting goal, we might want it all right now—whether it is the dream relationship, a new home, financial abundance, optimum health, the perfect job or our own business. But it rarely comes in one fell swoop. It tends to happen in smaller steps, which is actually a really good thing because it allows us to clarify and make finer distinctions as our dreams unfold and that ultimately brings us the best possible fit. So if you find yourself wanting to make it all happen now, you can stay connected to the excitement and anticipation whilst simply focusing on one small thing that moves you closer to your dreams today.

12th June
Expectations

People will *always* live up to our expectations of them. We give far too much credit to people for their behaviour towards us when it is actually our beliefs about them that is the determining factor. Have you noticed that one person can push your buttons yet be a wonderfully supportive friend to someone else? Or that person you admire and respect seems to offend or irritate another? The same people creating very different relationships—How can that be? In fact our beliefs and expectations *pull out* the behaviour of other people. If you consider someone to be selfish then guess what? —Selfish they will be! If you think someone is a loving person then loving they will be. So even if someone is giving you plenty of evidence to support your negative opinion of him or her today, try switching to a more positive view of how you would like them to be and you may just get a very pleasant surprise!

13th June
Superstitions

Are you superstitious? Do you avoid the cracks in the pavement, create seven years of worry when you crack a mirror or go into a head spin on Friday 13th? We need to remember that superstition is just another form of belief. We have so much cultural conditioning around these notions that even if we consciously reject the beliefs, often we unconsciously still hold onto a little bit of apprehension or anxiety that tends to be self-fulfilling. So no matter what superstitious encounters you have in your life, you can choose to believe that everything will always happen perfectly—and through the power of belief, you'll get to be right! Make the decision now to look for things that reinforce how well each and every day is going and filter out everything that doesn't fit with that! Whilst others are worrying and fretting, you will be on an upward spiral of success.

14th June
The Joy of Simplicity

Today the JoyScope reminds you of the joy of simplicity. Generally, we have a tendency to make things more difficult than they need to be. We take the long route to get the results we want because we have been misled that there is a certain way of doing things that we have to stick to. But there may be a shortcut that is hidden from view. What if you break the rules? What if you do it differently? What if you simplify your approach? Today pick an area of your life that feels like a chore—it could be managing financial records, paperwork or filing or just the weekly grocery shop. Consider how you could make it easier and more effective? A few minutes spent reviewing your strategies could bring even better results and free up valuable time and energy too! Simplicity is the key to experiencing space in your life.

15th June
Taking Action

Are you an action-taker? Many of us are hard wired to get things done in the least amount of possible time. We experience an issue or challenge in our lives and decide to tackle it head on. But that isn't always the most effective way of achieving results. Universal energy responds much more to our intention than to our action. In other words, if we take action from a place of fear or doubt hoping to rectify a problem, we transmit energy of neediness or desperation, which pushes away the very solution that we want. Instead, we need to ensure that we are aligned behind anything and everything we do. And the fastest way to come into alignment is by letting go of the need to control the outcome. That may mean making peace with the current situation but it is worth it. Otherwise we are simply pushing boulders up hills and eventually we tire of all that efforting. It's just easier to let it all go.

16th June
Your Mantra

Today the message from the JoyScope is to compose your own mantra! When we are in the process of lining ourselves up with something that we want having an affirmation to support us can be invaluable. You can choose anything that uplifts and inspires you and puts you in that feel-good place where the magic happens. If you are in a transition period, you may want to affirm *"I am letting go of the old to make way for the new"*. If you are right on track, you could affirm, *"I am enjoying and appreciating the journey"*. Or you may be excelling in your life right now and want to affirm *"The better it gets, the better it gets"*. Find your own mantra and dose yourself up with wonderful words of encouragement on a daily basis. Fully prescribed by the JoyScope!

17th June
Looking Ahead

When you're driving it's good to keep your eyes on the road ahead. It wouldn't work so well if you put your focus of attention on what you can see in the rear view mirror! In fact, it wouldn't take long for you to run into trouble. The same is true of life. When we continue to focus on things that have happened in the past, we deprive ourselves of all the wonderful things that are lining up in our future. So turn your attention to the road ahead. Keep your viewpoint fixed on where you are going and you are much more likely to enjoy the journey and, of course, it is much easier to spot the opportunities that you are heading towards.

18th June
Mindfulness

Do you ever have days when you feel you are working way too hard? Today is going to be the antidote to all that efforting. If you slow down and take your time, you may notice that you are achieving much more than you were when you were rushing and hurrying around. Practice mindfulness. Keep your focus on the task at hand and give it your undivided attention. Be in the moment and with your experience as it is. Let go of the need to be planning or thinking about what comes next. As you do, become aware of how much easier it is to get things done. Today will be an ultra-productive day!

19th June
Inputs and Outputs

The quality of our life is really a simple formula—inputs + outputs = life experience! Anytime we become unbalanced, the quality of our life will deteriorate. Inputs are made up of a number of different factors; nutrition, rest, information that we absorb—anything that we take in. Outputs on the other hand are where we expend our energy, which could be working, exercising, fulfilling our roles as a parent or caregiver—anything that we give out. When we are giving too much to the outside world, we feel stressed, exhausted and burnt out. When we have too much coming in, we may feel sluggish, overwhelmed or depressed. The key is to find ways to bring the self into balance. When you are able to identify what you need in every moment, to know when to nourish yourself and when to take action, life becomes a smooth and satisfying ride.

20th June
Body Wisdom

Your body is infinitely wise. There are many biological processes that you don't need to think about. Imagine how complicated life would get if you needed to remember to breathe! But in some cases, we have trained our bodies to behave differently and they don't function in an optimal way. But our body will offer guidance on what it needs moment by moment. Our job is simply to pay attention and listen carefully. So what does your body want today—a healthy nutritious meal or perhaps a treat? Some vigorous exercise or maybe some rest, refreshment and rejuvenation? Mental stimulation or quiet meditation? Trust the wisdom of your body and it will respond wonderfully, giving you the perfect indication of what it needs every time.

21st June
Willpower

Will power is hugely over-rated. Any time you are striving to achieve through will alone, you set up an inner struggle within yourself. A part of you wants to get it done, whist another part of you would prefer to choose something else! So, today, instead of using grit and determination to get you through, take time to connect to the purpose of what you are doing. What will the results bring for you in your life? Even the most mundane of jobs can have a higher purpose if you are willing to seek it out. When you are lined up with the benefits, will power becomes unnecessary. It is all about the joy of personal fulfillment instead.

22nd June
Turning It Over

Here is a little game for you to play today but only if you want to have some fun and achieve results effortlessly! Think of a challenge or issue that you are facing or just something you would like to improve. It could be an area of your life where you feel stuck as this works particularly well. Take a piece of paper and write down whatever it is that you would like to change and fold the paper. Then take an envelope and place the piece of paper inside and seal it. On the front of the envelope, simply write; "*I now turn this over to the Universe. I trust and let go*". Place the envelope somewhere safe and out of immediate sight. Now your work is done. You are turning this challenge over to the Universe, which always has the perfect solution. Your job is to get out of the way and let the magic happen. There will come a time in the future when you are drawn back to the envelope. Until then, let go of the need to intervene or make things happen and just allow Universal energies to do what is best. If you find yourself being drawn back to the issue, simply refocus and remind yourself that you have turned it over to the Universe. When we step aside, miracles can happen. Just watch and see!

23rd June
Inspired Parenting

Parenting is nothing short of a fine art. Balancing the need for boundaries and guidelines whilst allowing space for creative expression and play can be a challenge. Ultimately we want our children to grow up as happy and healthy individuals and for that they need to discover their own path in life. So how do we decide when to step in and intervene and when to hold back and let them find their own way? One approach is to simply consider the potential benefits and consequences. We wouldn't want our children to unnecessarily suffer but the odd mistake here and there can be a wonderful way to learn. So next time a difficult situation arises, don't fuss over small stuff. Ask yourself if this is a good opportunity for them to self-discover. When the answer is *"yes"*, take a step back and be the proud parent who gets to watch their child grow into their magnificent self.

24th June
Does It Matter?

Here's a question that you may want to add to your life questions: *"Does it really matter?"* How often do we find ourselves dwelling over something from the past or nervously anticipating something that may happen in the future and wasting our vital time and energy? We know that the past is done with and the future is uncertain so anything we are contemplating that is not about enjoying this moment just depletes our resources. Yes, we want to milk the good memories and joyfully expect the great times ahead but if it feels anything less than uplifting, just let it go. Asking yourself *"Does it really matter"* gives you a fresh perspective and often the opportunity to forget (and forgive if needs be!) Even if the answer seems to be *"yes"*, remember that in the direst of circumstances, things will always improve and they will get better much more quickly when your focus is on things that make you happy. And in the grand scheme of things, being happy is all that really matters.

25th June
Void of Silence

One of the biggest fears of public speaking is the thought of forgetting your words. Authors dread the experience of writers block. First dates are uncomfortable when neither party knows what to say. All of these have something in common. A fear of the blankness that accompanies *not knowing*. What an interesting quandary we create! Why is the void of silence such a scary proposition in these or any situation? Could we not just stop and be still for a while and wait and see what wants to be born next? Why is knowing perceived to be so much more valuable than embracing the delicious and expansive space of uncertainty. For in uncertainty, the purest of possibilities exists. Today the JoyScope invites you to drop into the void of silence and to discover the treasures that lie in not knowing. Encourage others to just sit and be with you in the silence and space. Stop speaking the words out and let the words find you within. Because in those words, you will find you!

26th June
Change Your Reaction

No matter how hard we try, we can't force someone to behave in a particular way. No amount of reasoning, explaining and rationalising will persuade someone to be the way you want them to be. If it is a stranger or brief acquaintance, the solution is easy—just turn around and walk away. But what if it is someone who is in your close circle: a friend, a family member or a work colleague? If you can't change them, you are left with the only other alternative—to change your reaction towards them. They may be the most annoying, frustrating and maddening person in the world, who definitely *should* change but you are wasting your time, energy and peace of mind when you want them to be different to how they are. Your ability to respond differently, to take the higher ground, to love them anyway (even if you don't like what they are doing), will not just transform your relationship with them but also bring more joy and happiness to your life too. You aren't doing it for them; you are doing it for you.

27th June
Life Phases

Our life will move through distinct phases. These are reflected in the changes in our life. It could be the start or end of a relationship, redundancy or a new job, the birth of a child or a house move. But some changes are even subtler. These show up as small shifts in our awareness and our way of being in the world. It is all part of our personal and spiritual development journey. Our willingness to recognise these shifts and to adjust our life to reflect the new phase is essential to our ongoing growth. Maybe there is something you have outgrown or are ready to let go of. Maybe there is a new desire or dream bubbling up inside of you. Listen to your inner guidance and if you experience a nudge in a new direction, be willing to make the change. When we listen to the whispers, the Universe doesn't need to shout!

28th June
Clutter Clear

This is a great time for some ruthless clutter clearing! We accumulate so much *stuff* on our journey through life and there is great value in having a sort out and letting go of that which we don't need or doesn't serve us any more. It's a wonderful boost for our energy and it sends a message to the Universe that we have space for the new and exciting things we desire to come in. Start small—clear out a drawer or a cupboard or simply tackle that filing you have been avoiding! As you begin to let go, the momentum will build and soon you will be totally unstoppable.

29th June
Life is a Playground

Have you ever stopped to watch children having fun in a playground? One minute they are swinging from monkey bars, another they are spinning on a merry-go-round and then they dive headlong into a sandpit to build castles and other wonderful creations. They flit from apparatus to activity, not worrying that they are missing out, because they know there is enough time and variety to keep the joy flowing. Life really isn't very different. Consider the diversity of life activities and equipment that we get to pick from. So many wonderful choices—how we earn a living, who we spend our time with, the places we can travel to and explore. What an amazing playground of possibilities we are blessed to have in our reach. So then the only question left to ask is *"What will you play with today"*?

30th June
Emotional Expression

Early in life we begin making decisions about how safe we feel when we share our deepest feelings. If we feel supported and understood, we grow up able to express our emotions without fearing repercussions. But, at some time, most of us have had an experience where our feelings have been over-ridden or simply not acknowledged and so we learn to repress those that we feel are unacceptable. Today, the JoyScope reminds you that all emotions are appropriate as they are simply your inner guidance pointing you in a certain direction. If you feel depressed, maybe you are being guided to take better care of your own needs. If you feel angry, maybe you need to speak out and have your wants and needs heard. Trust your emotional indicators and follow the direction that they point to. All paths can lead to happiness!

1st July
The Next Decade

Where were you ten years ago today? What was life like for you? Maybe it seems like just yesterday. Maybe is seems like a lifetime ago. Sometimes because of the way that time distorts, it can seem to be both at the same time! But whatever your answer, take a moment to ponder on how life has altered and changed for you. Not all of those changes may be exactly as you would want but the key thing to focus on is how you have evolved as a person. Life experiences teach us and make us wiser. As you reflect on your journey, notice the person you have become. Pay particular attention to all of the positive aspects of your personal growth. Now consider the future. If you were to repeat this process in ten years time, what would need to be true for you to be saying, *"That was a great decade"*? And as you think about that, whom do you need to become to create that experience. There is nothing that can stop you—unless you allow it. Remember, anything is possible!

2nd July
A Simple "*I Love You*"

Today the message from JoyScope is simple—remember to tell the special people in your life how much you love and cherish them. When we have busy lives and hectic schedules, it can be so easy to get caught up in all the events and actions on our to-do list that we forget to share our loving thoughts with the people close to us. We may think that it goes without saying but a simple "*I love you*" directed to a family member or friend reminds them how special they are. For when you come to the last moments of life, you will judge your life experience on the quality of your intimate relationships. You will remember those that mattered most. Don't they need to know that? So go on, make someone's day by sharing how much you care.

3rd July
Responsibility

We may have the best intentions in the world but we can't always predict the impact of what we say or do. To stay in perfect alignment, we have to recognise where our responsibility begins and ends. We can take ownership of our thoughts, our feelings and our beliefs. They all belong to us and us alone—just as the opinions and emotions of others belong to them. We have no control over what others think or feel. There is no blame, simply awareness. Blame comes from a victim standpoint that serves no one. Instead, we can develop our own self-awareness to know when we have slipped into judgments of others and when others are mistakenly projecting their responsibility on to us. When we own what is rightfully ours and gently let go of all that is not, we live a peaceful and tuned-in existence.

4th July
Overcoming Obstacles

Occasionally as we reach boldly for our dreams, we encounter obstacles. They may seem like temporary blips or insurmountable hurdles but even in the face of these setbacks, we have a choice of where to put our focus. If we continue to give our attention to the thing that stands in our way, we may feel thwarted or frustrated or hopeless. But as we keep our focus on our dreams, it allows the Universe to deliver a solution—that may be even better than the original plan! Today remember that everything continues to evolve. Trust the process and follow your dreams and allow the Universe to conspire to bring you what you really want.

5th July
Awakening Moods

How would you describe your mood when you wake in the morning? Are you joyful, excited and full of anticipation for the day ahead? Or perhaps a little less enthusiastic or worried about what will happen? Well the good news is that you can change your mood each and every day with a very simple process. At night, just before you settle down for a good night's sleep, take a few moments to vision the kind of day you want to have tomorrow. You can imagine everything flowing, chance coincidences and synchronicities bringing you more of what you want and exciting new opportunities coming your way. Even if there is something looming in your diary that seems less than positive, you can still imagine it going better that you could possibly expect right now. When we drift off to sleep with a positive mindset, we bring that energy through into the next day and wonderful things can happen. Sleep well tonight and enjoy the benefits tomorrow!

6th July
Curiosity

Where does true inspiration come from? Being able to access instant inspiration and creativity is a secret known to the best inventors, creatives and entrepreneurs. Yet it is something we can all discover and, once we know how, we can have these states of being at our disposal whenever we choose. Already curious? That's a great place to start! Curiosity is the perfect antidote to boredom. Whenever we are stuck in the familiar, life will feel flat and dull. To find your juice, explore the unknown. Spend time each and every day seeking out what is new and what is different. Rather than judging whether an experience is good or bad, instead simply ask yourself how it is dissimilar to all of the other experiences you have had. Not with the intent to take any particular action, just with the willingness to let life inspire you. Curiosity has been known to open up new worlds of possibilities.

7th July
Beyond Ego

The message from the JoyScope today is to remember that we are much more than we think ourselves to be. Our thoughts are often unconsciously driven by our ego, which has a limited perspective and awareness of life. Anxiety, worry, guilt and regret are just emotional patterns generated by our fearful ego that likes to think it is in control. But a whole new level of control emerges when we are prepared to gently challenge our limited thinking and acknowledge the real truth. Beyond your ego, you are pure potential, with the ability to handle anything that life throws at you. Listen to the voice of awareness rather than the voice of ego and discover the riches of life.

8th July
Comfort Zones

Are you a comfort zone junkie? When was the last time you really stepped out of your comfort zone and tried something new? As we mature, it becomes a little too easy to fall into conservative patterns of behaviour—doing the same kinds of things in the same sort of way. Today do something different! It could be something big like signing up for that once in a lifetime adventure or something small like taking a different route to work. It really doesn't matter! Variety expands the mind and creates new opportunities and possibilities. One small step in a different direction can create magical ripples throughout your life.

9th July
States of being

There are really only two states of being—resisting or allowing. When we are in the mode of resistance, life feels like hard work and requires effort to get things done. But our most natural state is one of allowing. When we are allowing, things will happen automatically and magically. Whatever we want or need seems to just miraculously appear. So, today let go of the resistance in your life. If things don't go according to plan, try saying *"Ah well"* and remind yourself that all will be well again very soon. As we release the battle with our current reality, we move into a more allowing state that enables what we want to show up.

10th July
Honour Your Heart

The message from JoyScope today is to honour your heart. Remember that it is always okay to have desires and needs, no matter how trivial or far-fetched they may seem. Too many of us have squished our dreams in the face of opposition or ridicule. Now is the time to awaken the desire once more. So what is your heart asking for you? Listen carefully to the secrets it shares and honour each and every request. When your heart speaks, it pays to take note. As you listen to the guidance from your heart, you will discover that it already knows the route to your most inspired life. Trust and be good to your heart and it will be a wonderful servant for life.

11th July
Impatience

There are times in our lives when things appear to be moving slowly or even not at all! When we have a big dream or strong desire, we may feel impatient that it is not happening quickly enough. But life is always progressing at exactly the right pace and in exactly the right way. Trust that the Universe is lining you up with everything that you want. And once that alignment has happened, things are likely to move very quickly indeed. Delight in the positive expectation of all that is on the way. Make the anticipation as thrilling and exciting as the actual manifestation of your dream. Once you can truly and completely enjoy this phase, it is bound to show up—really fast!

12th July
Changing Contexts

We know that one of the keys to living an inspired life is forward momentum. But what happens when you aren't able to move forwards in an area of your life? It may be because you are waiting for additional information or for someone to make a decision that affects you or simply just because you lack clarity on what to do next. How do we keep that momentum going? The simplest way to continue moving forwards is to change context. Unsure about a relationship situation— then maybe you can spend time nurturing your inner relationship. Weighed down by financial burdens— then perhaps look to enhance or improve your health and wellbeing. Career seems to be stalling—Could you take up a new hobby? Even if it seems that parts of our lives are stuck, we can still invite creativity and inspiration in by directing our energy into other areas of life. And the good news is that as we move forwards purposefully, life will continue to evolve to meet us.

13th July
Feeling Feelings

Do you enjoy feeling good? Whether it is happiness or joy or bliss or peace, everyone enjoys basking in those good vibes and most of us would like to be able to intensify those feelings and have more of them every day. Why wouldn't we? The problem is that when we feel less good, we are much less willing to experience those feelings fully. Instead, we tend to detach from those emotions we label as negative like anger, frustration, sadness and grief. And we do that by cutting off from our hearts and escaping into our logical and rational minds. But you can't have one without the other. When we cut off the bad feelings, we cut off the good ones too and that sets us up for flat lining through life. We can only really feel when we are in our bodies, fully experiencing the world. Take time to do things that bring you into your body completely. Whether it is a massage, physical exercise or even a hug. There is nothing more important for an inspired and happy life.

14th July
Your Theme Tune

What is the theme tune for your life? Music can have a very powerful influence on how we are feeling. We don't always pay a lot of attention to the choices of music we listen to, yet it has the ability to take us into wallowing or self-pity (think Bridget Jones singing "*All by myself*") or to raise and lift our spirit. So as you think about your life, what would be your choice of track? Even if life isn't exactly how you would want it to be right now, there is a good selection of inspiring music that is a match for where you want to be heading (even if it is D-ream's, "*Things can only get better*"). Pick a track today that feeds your soul and make it the theme tune for your life.

15th July
Trust Yourself

Do you trust yourself? Trusting yourself is about having faith in your ability to make decisions and take action that is right for you. Given that we spend *all* of our time with our *self*, it is a little surprising that we don't always know what we want. The good news is that even when you aren't totally sure consciously, unconsciously you always know what will move you in the direction of your dreams and what will take you the wrong way. To access this inner wisdom, we just need to learn to tune into ourselves. Create some space and sit gently with ideas and inspirations. Guidance can come in many forms, pictures and symbols, an internal voice or nudge, or feelings and sensations in our bodies. When we take the time to listen, our guidance will speak—clearly!

16th July
Agreement

Today the message from the JoyScope is to practice being *in agreement* with others. When we are collaborating with everyone, our energy can flow more effectively and it invites other cooperative situations and people into our lives. That's not to say we need to compromise completely and ignore our own desires. It's important to speak up about what we want and honour our preferences. But there is usually a win-win alternative, if we are prepared to keep working to find a better option. Instead of wanting to defend our position, seeking the best outcome is a much better use of our time and resources. The good news is that very often, at the heart of the matter, there is a common ground that can be used as a platform for creating the perfect solution.

17th July
Emotional Baggage

Airlines have a very strict limit on the weight of luggage that they will allow you to check in. When you exceed the limit, they charge you heavily in excess fees. Life isn't really that dissimilar. When we are carrying emotional baggage, it weighs us down and costs us dearly in terms of our energy, vitality and happiness. So, today, let's pretend you are at life's check in. Your clerk has weighed your bags and you have exceeded the allowed limit of emotional luggage. Open all of those cases and bags containing your past experiences and memories. Where are you holding onto negative emotion that isn't serving you? What are you ready to let go of? Imagine that you can pull out all of that unnecessary excess and simply discard it. Most of it was probably other people's stuff anyway! Experience the relief of lightening the load and feel the freedom of travelling light.

18th July
Intuition

We often talk about intuition as though it is just a gut feeling we have about certain things, like a person we feel unsure around or a decision where we are swayed one way for no logical reason. All of that is part of our intuitive awareness but true intuition is even more than that. Have you ever been thinking about someone that you haven't seen for a while and then almost miraculously you run into them or they call out of the blue? Maybe you have been in conversation with someone and known what they are going to say before they even opened their mouths? Our intuition exists beyond the boundaries and limitations of time and space. We have the ability to tap into this sixth sense and allow our intuition to guide us towards our dreams. The question is: *will you let go of the need to analyse and rationalise and simply trust?*

19th July
Acceptance

There is great power in accepting things just as they are. Its good to have our dreams and desires but when we make our current reality wrong in some way, we can't experience happiness. So today the message from the JoyScope is to find peace in acceptance. Know that nothing needs to change for you to experience the happiness that you truly deserve. The paradox is that when you stop fighting for things to be different, you may actually find that you start to notice many reasons to be happy, previously hidden from view. Acceptance can be powerful like that!

20th July
Feeding Our Senses

Have you ever wondered why our society is so predisposed to suffer headaches? Our current culture encourages us to spend a lot of time in our heads—processing data, using logic, reasoning and analysing. Whilst these are essential life skills, the real joy of living comes from being fully present to our life experiences, using all of the five senses—sight, hearing, smell, taste and touch. When we are delighting our senses, we experience feelings of balance, stability and solidity. So spend some time today feeding your senses. It could be inspiring music, physical exertion, painting, smelling the roses or a gourmet meal of delicious taste-tingling food. Live a sensual life and boundless satisfaction will be your reward.

21st July
Self-expectation

Do you have high expectations of yourself? Notice that there is a big difference between driving towards your goals in an attempt to prove your worthiness, and having high expectations because you just *know* you are capable of so much. When we reach for the best we can be, it feels exciting and fulfilling. We begin to release our untapped potential. Our perception of who we are continues to evolve and causes our life to expand proportionally. Where will your self-expectation take you today? Unleash the best of you on everyone today. Take the world by storm!

22nd July
Role Models

Who has made a significant difference in your life? As you reflect back, who was there at a turning point or supported you through a transition? Was there someone who changed the course of your life and ensured that things were never the same again? Who are you thankful to? Do they know? Make this day the day that you find them and express your appreciation. Even if you are no longer in touch, you can seek them out or simply picture them in your mind's eye. Not only will it make you both feel good but also you never know where the conversation will lead. Appreciation is a powerfully transformative energy and when we allow it to flow, we invite more similar experiences to be thankful for into our life.

23rd July
Inspiration Place

Do you have an inspiration place? An inspiration place is somewhere you can go and just know that the ideas and insights will flow. For some people, this maybe a quiet place outside in nature. For others, it might be a bustling coffee bar surrounded with friends. Whenever we feel stuck, taking some time to visit our inspiration place is a great way to get back into the flow of life. And we don't have to wait to feel out of sorts. Creating regular *time-outs* is the perfect way to sustain an inspired life. When we nurture our minds and spirits, we invite creativity and focus into our lives. And that is an exceptionally powerful combination.

24th July
Tenacity

Some of the best ideas take time to come into fruition. Numerous publishers turned down J K Rowling before *Harry Potter* was accepted. Thomas Edison had a vision for the light bulb but it took multiple attempts to find a suitable filament, and Colonel Sanders' recipe for fried chicken was rejected over and over again before he was successful. What do all of these people have in common? Persistence and tenacity. Being turned down was never a failure, just evidence that they were closer to bringing their dream into reality. When you consider your dreams, are you prepared to go the extra mile? Will you stick with it, even if others say "*no*"? Are you prepared to hold onto your vision in the face of adversity? Your ability to believe will always be the determining factor in your success.

25th July
Pause for Preparation

There's a great deal to be said for good preparation. Yet when we talk about preparing, we probably think of action plans and to-do lists. How often do we really consider preparing ourselves for the situation? How much time do we give ourselves to get into the right mood or emotional state to make the most of our experiences? If our lives are busy, we may be running from appointments to commitments without taking the space to pause in between. It could be that we arrive at work, still reeling from a family disagreement or we come home to our family with a mind full of work challenges. We struggle to stay present when talking with loved ones and friends or we go to bed with the weight of the day still hanging heavy and have a sleepless and restless night. Today master the art of pausing. Take just a few moments between each event and experience to bring all of your attention back into the moment. Be all of you in every situation and the quality of your life will dramatically and instantly improve.

26th July
Get Jiggy With It!

The message from the JoyScope today is that this is a great time to *get jiggy with it*! Far too often we can find ourselves plodding through the day or at the mercy of the ever growing to do list. So why not make it different? Dance, waltz, skip and strut your way to an uplifting day. Put your favourite CD on whilst you work or are doing housework or just do nothing else but move your body along to the music. A bit of boogieing goes a very long way to instant inspiration. Dance your way to a happy life!

27th July
Dare to Take a Risk

Sometimes you need to take a risk in life. It may feel a bit scary and overwhelming but you know it is right when you get bubbles of anticipation and excitement when you think about what the outcome could be. So what is the risk you are ready to take? It could be just a small step or a giant leap into the unknown. It may be a gamble but if you never try, you will never know and unfulfilled dreams are often much harder to live with than the prospect of making a mistake. Even if it doesn't work out, you are bound to learn from the experience. So be brave and go for it. Dare you!

28th July
Freedom

Do you want to be free? The basis of freedom is our ability to manage our state whatever the situation we are facing. When a problem occurs, if we immediately move into trying to solve it and don't give attention to how we are feeling first, the issue will always expand. Take a moment to breathe and experience the emotion. When you take time to acknowledge your feelings without judgment and then work on coming back into alignment with what you really want, you create the space for the best solution to appear. And as you change your state, any challenges will automatically transform. Today put your alignment before any action and notice how easy life gets.

29th July
Worst Case Scenario

What do you fear most? This may be a less than comfortable question to consider but it can also be totally transformative. Our fears are anticipations of things that *might* happen in the future, not things that are happening in the moment. When we are faced with the real deal, we will find that we have the resources to deal with it. Yet we torture ourselves with fearful thoughts about what could occur and how awful it would be. So the invitation from the JoyScope today is to face your fears full on. Imagine that the worst-case scenario did happen. Notice that either way, you would still be okay and that the world will keep spinning! Challenge the thoughts that take away your power and let peace flood in.

30th July
Synchronicities

You may well be noticing strange happenings today. Synchronicity can be an amazing thing when you line up with being in the right place at the right time—a chance meeting, an unexpected opportunity or a wonderful surprise. But if you are experiencing events that are less than uplifting, just notice if you are holding on to any blocked emotions. Every time you experience something unwanted, if you just take a moment to notice how you feel as it occurred, you might notice a pattern emerging. If the emotional pattern is similar, ask yourself where that emotion is strongest and work on letting those thoughts go. As you do, you will notice that you let go of negative cycles and allow more of the good stuff to flow your way.

31st July
Importance Matters

What is the most important thing in your life? How did you answer? Maybe your partner, your children or your closest friends? If that is the case, do you really prioritise in a way that demonstrates your answer? Do the people who matter most always come first or do your allow your relationships to slide when outside factors are demanding your attention. Today put what matters most first. Let those people know the important role they have in your lives. Problems and issues will come and go. It is your rock solid relationships that will continue—so long as you nurture them with love and tenderness.

1st August
Building Your Tribe

It is said that you become like the people you spend most of your time with. That's a thought worth considering. Do you have a tribe of life-affirming and positive people who are there to cheer you on or rally around when you are down? It doesn't mean you have to ditch any of your friends but just become aware of the nature of the conversations you have. It can be validating to share your story with a confidante and have them empathise with your situation but just notice if those discussions turn into wallowing or self-pity. Ask your tribe to be the people who encourage you to go beyond what you think you are capable of. Find the people who never cease to see your potential. If you are to become like them, your evolution depends on it.

2nd August
Releasing Attachment

Have you ever noticed that when you really, really want something to happen it often doesn't yet when you stop thinking about it, it miraculously appears? A bit like the analogy of waiting for a bus for ages and then as soon as one shows up, a run of buses appear! When we want something and nothing is happening, it is usually our attachment to having it that causes the problem. So today, if there is something you really want, turn it over to the Universe and trust that it is handled. As you get out of your own way, you allow the good things to find their way to you.

3rd August
Life Dares

Today you are invited to tap into your courage. What have you wanted to do, maybe for a really long time, but have been avoiding? Perhaps it is starting your own business or applying for a dream job or promotion or signing up for a big challenge like a parachute jump or a marathon. Maybe you would like to go to university or enroll at night school. Perhaps extend your connections by joining a new group, a dating agency or asking *that* person out for a date! What would you love to do if you could pluck up the courage? These are our *life dares*— moments when we step beyond our self-imposed limitations and reach out to discover what is possible. As we do, we expand our boundaries and fast track our personal growth. Beyond our fear is the passion and excitement for life. So go on, be brave and step out today, you may just discover a whole lot more juice for your life.

4th August
Back to Now

Have you noticed that it can feel wonderful to anticipate the good things that are coming your way (for example, an event or holiday to look forward to) yet it can feel really awful when there is something on the horizon that fills you with dread or anxiety. So the message today is to only focus into the future and anticipate what is coming when it feels good. If there is something you are not looking forward to or you have fears about what might happen, you are going too far into the future. Gently pull your attention back to the now and keep your focus firmly on what is right in front of you. Most of the things that we dread are never so bad in reality! When we stay in now, we save so much wasted energy.

5th August
Widen Your Possibilities

The message from the JoyScope today is to widen your possibilities! Whenever we are faced with decisions or choices, it can be a little too easy to narrow down our options to just a couple of things—we can have this or we can have that! But there are actually always an infinite number of possibilities if we allow ourselves to expand our boundaries about what we believe can happen. So today, if you have the opportunity to make a choice, try imagining even bigger and better. What could you create if you knew no limits? And what happens when you stretch yourself beyond all of that? Break through the self-imposed limitations and have a wonderfully expansive day!

6th August
Changing States

Today the JoyScope is asking you to change states! How do you want to feel? Happy, peaceful, loving, connected, inspired, passionate, purposeful, relaxed, excited or ecstatic?

Or maybe it's something different for you? Or a combination of them all? Our emotions are not dependent on anything external in our environment. We don't need anything to change or be a certain way in order for us to feel good. How can that be possible? If you recall a time now when you felt truly inspired—notice what you are doing, who you are there with, what you can see, hear and feel. What happens? In order to recall a time when you felt a certain emotion, you have to recreate the feeling on the inside. But nothing has had to change on the outside for your feelings to change. Make a list of all the good states you would like to experience and make a choice to go there now. The only downside is that feeling good is hugely addictive and you may find that once you start, you just can't stop!

7th August
Uplifters

Are there people in your life who inspire you? Often, we are surrounded by *uplifters* who help us to stay focused on our dreams. These uplifters tend to sneak into people's lives under the disguise of friendship. They have a unique ability to reconnect you to your deepest desires or to say or do something in the moment that transforms challenges into opportunities. Perhaps as you reflect on your life, you notice one or two uplifters working behind the scenes to inspire your life. If so, take the time today to let these people know what they mean to you. A little bit of appreciation goes a long way. As you appreciate their presence and gifts, you become a match for more wonderful people to come into your life. The JoyScope is sure that you will agree—you can never have too many inspirational friends.

8th August
Committing to Life

Are you completely committed to your life? The changes in our culture have created massive uncertainties spreading into our careers, relationships and our well-being. As a result of our fears about what may or may not happen, we can end up guarding ourselves from disappointment or holding parts of ourselves back. But commitment is a powerful energy that has transformative effects on the quality of our life. We do nothing to enrich our experiences when we are only partly there. There is nothing that could happen that you aren't able to handle. Jump into life, fully immerse yourself and enjoy the richness that life has to offer. Make the commitment to live fully today.

9th August
Hug Day!

Today the JoyScope invites you to have a hug day. Who in your life deserves a cuddle? Maybe someone who stands by you and gives unwavering support when you need it most? Or a friend who is having a bad day and needs a pick-me-up? Or a child with a scraped knee or wounded emotions? When we hug, we break down the physical barriers that separate us and, in that moment, we connect as one. Hug freely and feel the aliveness in the connection. All hugs count on hug day!

10th August
Lottery Winning

Have you ever dreamt of winning the lottery? What amount of money would be a life-changing sum for you? A few thousand? A million? More? What difference would it make to your life? With your winnings, how could you contribute more fully to the lives of others? What else could you—would you—do? Doesn't the thought feel exciting and inspiring? But stop for just a moment and think. Why do you pin your hopes of abundance on the lottery? Perhaps it is because you don't yet have the faith that the Universe is able to bring you everything that you want with or without that lottery win! Each and every day, you are buying a lucky ticket to your dreams and it is a dead cert—all you need to do is simply trust and keep moving forwards.

11th August
Living Your Day

How do you live your day? It's worth taking a moment or two to really reflect on this question: How do you *live* your day? In other words, are you fully present to each and every moment? There is so much noise and distraction surrounding us that it is a little too easy to pulled in different directions. Our minds wander forwards to the future worrying about what might happen or are too busy focusing on our past and lamenting or regretting what has happened or not happened. So today, just be present to your life as it is right now, without judgment or criticism of your self or others.

Simply become the witness to all that you have and all that you are in this moment and watch as a world of possibilities and ease opens up to you.

12th August
A-ha's

Have you ever experienced an "*A-ha*" moment—A time when you gained a new understanding after which life was never the same again? Maybe it was something you watched or something you read or even a conversation with someone where a particular insight changed your perspective on life. Our current view is always limited because we simply cannot know all there is to know. When new information comes in, it causes our perspective to expand. With this new perspective, we have a different vantage point on life but it is still limited. So today's invitation from JoyScope is to expand your horizons. Allow yourself to have a wider view on your experiences and your life. What have you not been noticing fully until now? How many a-ha moments can you create today?

13th August
Speaking Out

Today the JoyScope wants to remind you that it's okay to speak your truth. Whilst we may aspire to be the most loving we can be towards others, we also need to honour and respect our own boundaries. Being authentic is essential for high quality relationships not just with other people, but also our inner relationship too! So take the time today to acknowledge what is most important to you and let others know and share in that. Through gently communicating our truth to others, we allow them to understand and connect with us even more deeply. Speaking up and speaking out fosters authentic and genuine relationships—the kind that are really worth having.

14th August
Break the Rules

The message from the JoyScope today is to be prepared to break the rules! Some of the best inventions have happened because the creator was prepared to step outside the norms and do something different. When the concept for steam engines was first explored, the idea was dismissed because it was thought that air would be forced into people at such great speeds that their lives would be put at risk. Bizarre as it may seem now, just consider how different our lives would have been if the rules hadn't be broken. Imagination blossoms when we are prepared to look past how things should be in order to discover what could be instead. Allow your mind to run riot today. There is nothing that isn't possible when you go beyond the limits.

15th August
The Power of Jealousy

Have you ever suffered from a case of the green-eyed-monster? Maybe you see someone who has the object of your desire (whether money, relationship, job, or status symbol) and in the moment you feel the pang of envy.

Jealousy is a natural human response that lets us know that we have an *un-manifested* dream or goal. It can be really valuable information as long as we gently acknowledge the desire within, rather than lamenting what we don't yet have! Consider any areas of your life where envy strikes and notice what you are focusing upon. Then turn your attention to the object of your desire, imagine it being a part of your life and then allow yourself to feel the thrill of pure, positive anticipation. Expect it to be so and so it will be.

16th August
I'll Be Happy When

Many of us fall into the trap of living the *"I'll be happy when..."* pattern. In one or more areas of our life, we place our focus on the idea that our lives will be better when we experience some kind of imagined future—*"I'll be happy when I meet The One"*, *"I'll relax when I have more money"*, *"I'll feel like I have more time for me when I get that promotion"* and so on. In doing so, not only do we hold ourselves apart from feeling good in the moment but we also set up an interesting phenomenon. Whilst we are reaching for a perceived future, we take ourselves out of our body. Our minds are living a future experience but (unless we have mastered time travel) our physical bodies have to remain in now. In other words, not only do you stop yourself from feeling the emotional response you think you will have when you reach that end goal, you also prevent yourself from feeling pretty much anything. You need to be in your body to have access to all of your wonderful feelings. Of course, you will have goals or intentions but being present and grounded is where you will discover the real passion and fun of life.

17th August
Healthy Eating

There is a wealth of information on healthy eating available. But, when you begin to research, you find that much of it is confusing and often contradictory. So how do you work out what to eat, when and how? What if your body already knew the answer? Wouldn't that make life so much easier? In fact, your body always knows what is right for you in each and every moment when we tune into it. So today, have fun with discovering your body's nutritional desires. Whether you are in a restaurant or in the shopping market, see if you can tap into your own body wisdom. It usually comes as a gentle nudge or guidance inside, often from the stomach area. You know when it is body guidance because all the *shoulds* and *should-nots* disappear. Maybe you will choose the salad or vegetables or maybe you will choose a treat or an indulgence. Stay tuned to what your body wants and you will never go far wrong.

18th August
Dream Experiences

What would be your dream experience? Perhaps the holiday of a lifetime, a promotion at work or maybe the most romantic event of your life? Whatever it is, notice that you can always create it in your mind's eye. You can choose to lament the fact that it isn't here yet or you can design your very own mental movie in glorious technicolour with the full soundscape! When you act *as if* you are already living it, not only do you send a clear message to the Universe about what you want, you also get to experience the richness of emotions and feelings that accompany the having of it right now. And then you also significantly increase the possibility of it showing up for real. Have fun being the director of your mind movies today.

19th August
Attractive Qualities

Have you ever noticed that you can really want something and not get it yet something you are non-plussed about shows up in your life straight away? How frustrating! Do you think that is because you are cursed in some way or maybe down to a different factor? It can't be the amount of desire behind your request because clearly your wanting is much greater in the first instance. And before you start thinking that it is because you are unlucky, jinxed or suffering from bad karma, please be reassured that it is none of those things either. Desire is only part of the equation. Manifestation doesn't just require you to know what you want but also to have a deep and unwavering faith that it is on its way. Without trust, our desires turn to desperation and our dreams will continue to elude us. Desperation repels rather than attracts. You can have whatever you want. It's already there waiting for you. Trust and faith are the most attractive qualities we will ever possess!

20th August
Time Management

Traditional time management teaches us that we should spend more time working on the important things rather than getting bogged down in the things that are urgent yet less significant. It certainly makes sense and can help us to lead productive and purposeful lives. But what happens when it all becomes important *and* urgent! When we have too much to do in too little time, it is easy to get overwhelmed or frozen in procrastination. The answer—just take one small step at a time. When everything seems to have the same priority then it really doesn't matter what you pick. Just pick something, give it your full and undivided attention (without distracting yourself with the rest of the to-do list) and enjoy the satisfaction of getting it done. Then pick another and another and another. Small steps quickly lead to huge momentum.

21st August
Underdogs

In our culture, there is an unhealthy pattern in the media that we are probably all familiar with. The classic *build 'em up, knock 'em down pattern* has seen the rise and fall of many a would-be celebrity from underdog to idol and then to object of ridicule, often in the name of entertainment! We may think that it doesn't affect us, that the people concerned have invited any torment into their lives. But beneath the surface, as we are caught up in the story, we are hypnotising ourselves to believe the hype. At the unconscious level we are internalising beliefs—that success can only be short-lived and that if we stick our head above the parapet, we will get knocked back down. These limiting thoughts will hold us back. Today the JoyScope challenges you to champion everyone that you watch, hear or read about. Seek out the best in others and shout it from the rooftops. In doing so, you teach yourself that it is safe to be all of who you are. We are meant to step out and shine!

22ⁿᵈ August
Refreshing Sleep

Our well-being relies on certain foundations. Nutritious food, regular exercise and restful sleep are essential components to feeling good. Just as we can choose our diet and make time to move our bodies, we can also program ourselves to have sleep that is rejuvenating. Tonight, when you are ready, take time to pull your energy back from all the people, projects and demands on your time and attention. Spend a few moments reflecting and appreciating the best bits of the day (and if it's not been a good day, you can simply be grateful that it's a new day tomorrow!) Then ask your inner guidance to help you to sleep soundly and peacefully. Check if there is anything you need to let go of or park to free up your mind. When we take the time to set ourselves up for a good night's sleep, we maximize the chance that it will be effective and restful. And then we wake tomorrow with renewed energy and vigour for life.

23rd August
Giving Freely

One of the most rewarding things we can do is to give to another person without any expectation of receiving something in return. This doesn't mean giving out of a sense of obligation, rather making a deliberate choice to donate our time and attention from a place of love and connectedness. The cause of most of life's resentment is a sense that when we give, it is not reciprocated. So many arguments in relationships with loved ones and friends stem from the feeling of being taken for granted. But when you make giving freely your objective, the feel-good benefits come from the process of giving and not from the expectations of return. Giving freely sets you free!

24th August
Uniqueness

There is no one in this world quite like you—no one has the exact same personality, no one has had the same experiences as you and no one knows all that you know. So that makes you totally unique. There never has been and never will be another you. How breathtaking is that? Just by being you, you already make a unique contribution to the planet. The world just wouldn't be the same without you! So with all of that in mind, how do you want to express your uniqueness? There are no rules—you get to decide how you would like to shine. Just make sure you do. Your planet needs you!

25th August
This Now!

What day is it today? Are you sure? How do you know? Really ask yourself— how do you know what day it is? I'm sure most people will have been able to identify the day fairly easily and instantly. Even when we lose track of dates, like when we are on holiday, it doesn't take much calculation in order to figure it out. But what about the question of how you know it is that date? If you consider that deeply, it may be less easy to answer. In fact, days of the week are a form of consensus reality. In order to know time (a man-made invention) and therefore what is past and what is present, we need a structure we can concur upon. So we agree on hours in the day, days of the week and months of the year and so on. Of course this is useful because it means that we can arrange to meet or gather at a particular point in time— imagine trying to plan an outing if there was no structure of hours, days or months! But we must also be aware that these are completely constructed. You see there has never been and will never be a different time that is not now. We exist, we live, and we function only in this moment, this now. And if now is all there really is, then how can there ever be any worry, anxiety, guilt or blame? Today, as you go about your business, take time to remind yourself that the source of all of your living is only in this now!

26th August
Acknowledging Emotions

Living an inspired life is a balancing act. The Law of Attraction says that in order to manifest what we desire, we have to become a match vibrationally for what we want. That means staying focused on the positives and filtering our experience for the positive aspects and attributes. Yet when we become too hung up on staying positive that can have a detrimental effect too. It is absolutely about choosing to ignore the unwanted but when we deny our true feelings and try to act positive whilst our emotions are telling us something different, we are only fooling ourselves. The Law of Attraction will continue to bring us what we are vibrationally in alignment with rather than what we hope for. From time to time, we may need to face a gremlin or two. We may be challenged to deal with beliefs or thought patterns that continue to hold us back. When we find that we can't simply turn around because something unwanted has our attention, then we just need to be gentle and soothe that part of us that is fearful or sad or angry. When we take care of our emotions, our emotions take care of us.

27th August
Media Distortion

Do you believe everything you read in the newspapers and watch on TV? The news is created for dramatic effect and is made up of a collection of worst-case scenarios. It can be too easy to buy into the messages and allow our view of the world to become distorted. In truth, we live in a wonderful and exciting world with many opportunities and adventures to be had. All that is good so far outweighs anything negative—it just doesn't seem news worthy. So today, let's make a stand against media distortion. Why not put down the paper and switch off the TV and celebrate all that is good. Your life will be all the better for it!

28th August
Renegotiating Commitments

The theme for today's JoyScope is renegotiating commitments. When we live with integrity, it is natural for us to honour our commitments to other people. However, our circumstances are always changing and evolving and it may be that a commitment you made in the past no longer works for you. When you notice that it isn't serving you, it is perfectly reasonable to renegotiate the contract. When we try to keep a promise that is no longer in our higher and best interests, we are not honouring ourselves and that takes us out of the flow. Living with integrity is a willingness to always be authentic and honest. It is trusting that if the decision to change something is right for us, it has to be right for the other person. Sometimes, when we speak up and *un-commit*, we actually give the other person the gift of finding a solution that is a much better match for them. It is okay to change your commitments—permission is granted!

29th August
Mastery

When we take on new tasks or projects, we require our brains to cope with unfamiliar information. Every piece of additional knowledge or skill takes time to embed and become automatic. But we don't always plan for this and it can lead us to feel overwhelmed—too much new data is bombarding our senses. It is wonderful to have dreams and ambitions and to be moving forward with purpose. However, we need to balance this with space to reflect and catch our breath. Our minds have a huge capacity for dealing with many things simultaneously, but each new thing requires a little more brainpower and energy. So today the message from the JoyScope is to be gentle with your mind. Give it the space and time it deserves to learn and integrate and you will be rewarded with mastery.

30th August
Crisis to Awakening

Transitions and transformation are a part of life. Everything around us is *always* changing and we are no exception to the rule. Occasionally, those changes become full blown crises when everything that we have come to know seems to crumble and disintegrate around us. It can be an unsettling and frightening time. But a crisis is just a form of awakening, if we are able to embrace it rather than try to ignore it or run from it or seek to *fix* it. In a moment of crisis, the inner conflict we have been experiencing unconsciously temporarily reveals itself to our conscious awareness. It is a real gift. When we are willing to gently allow the crisis to show us the truth, we come to a new level of understanding about ourselves that will truly enrich our lives. Are you ready to welcome crises as the door to a whole new you?

31st August
Sing Your Song

There is a saying that is often quoted: *"Don't die with the music still in you"*. We all have unique and special gifts that deserve to be shared. How many times do we witness an undiscovered star seize a window of opportunity and deliver a musical performance that takes our breath away? Wouldn't it have been a tragedy if that voice had remained unheard? You might not be a musician but you still have a voice and that voice is best expressed when we show up in the world as our authentic self. When we hide our special talents, we deprive others of experiencing our gifts. Your voice matters to the world. Just by being you, you can inspire and influence others. So what is the music that wants to be played through you? Sing your song today.

1st September
Joyful Journeys

The joy of living is not about reaching the end destination—the real pleasure is found in the journey. We all have desires. They may be small goals or big dreams. If we make our happiness dependent on achieving results, we hold ourselves apart from feeling good now. But we can be happy just by enjoying the experience of reaching for what we want. Today, whether you think things are going to plan or not, give yourself permission to be happy. Maybe things will work out in exactly the way you want, maybe things will turn out differently or maybe things will end up being better than you ever imagined. Stand back and let everything unfold in just the right way. And in the meantime, concentrate on feeling good. The joy of the journey is the zest of life.

2nd September
Whispers from Your Soul

The message from the JoyScope today is to trust what you are drawn to do, even if it doesn't seem relevant. Our higher self knows exactly what is right for us and will gently nudge us in the right direction. These are the whispers from your soul, and good things happen when you trust this voice within. Sometimes we ignore these subtle suggestions. We notice the inclination to pursue a certain path and quickly reject it as a crazy or irrelevant thought. Yet there may be great wisdom hidden within the idea. You may be prompted to visit a place you wouldn't normally go or to take an action you wouldn't normally take. When we trust these messages and are willing to do something out of the ordinary, even if it seems ridiculous, we line ourselves up with magical moments.

3rd September
Beyond Perfection

Do you ever find yourself striving for perfection? Whilst holding ourselves to a high standard is important, often we can get paralyzed in thinking that something needs to be perfect. When we strive too hard or for too long, we waste valuable energy and get locked into a pattern of things never quite being good enough. In doing so, we regularly deprive ourselves of good feelings like satisfaction and fulfillment. So, today, ask yourself whether you are pushing for excellence or driving for perfection? If you notice that you fall into the second category, release the need for it to be faultless. Check in and see—it may already be good enough. And remember, you certainly are good enough just as you are. So take the opportunity to remind yourself that you are always perfect. Perfectly you!

4th September
Life's Adventures

Remember what it was like to be a child when your curiosity would turn you into an avid explorer trying lots of new things in lots of new ways? When did that all change? Life is a great big adventure. There are so many things to discover and enjoy. We miss out on all the fun when we limit the potential of what we think we can do. So what adventures would you like to have on this planet? Where would you like to go? What would you like to see? Become a life adventurer again and explore this wonderful and mysterious world.

5th September
Defensiveness

Do you ever find yourself getting defensive? Maybe someone says something you don't agree with or perhaps you feel you have a just cause to protect. Taking a defensive stance rarely brings us what we want. In the moment that we push back against someone or something, we give away our own peace of mind. It's not about being a pushover and taking everything that is thrown our way but there are other states of being that are much more likely to generate the outcome we want. When we stay in a place of understanding, trust and alignment, often we find that the issues we were pushing back on seem to miraculously disappear.

6th September
Evolution

Our lives will always be evolving. Those things that were right for us once become outdated and no longer serve our highest and best interests. Things that were once an integral part of our lives no longer fit with the person we are now. It may be a relationship or a job or the place that we live. But more often, it is simply a way of being in the world. On our path to awakening we will move through many different phases. We must be willing to let go, sometimes plunging into the unknown, in order to continue our evolution. What is no longer serving you? Perhaps a habit or a lifestyle choice? Gently release that which holds you back and embrace the path to a whole new you.

7th September
Boundaries

How effective are your personal boundaries? Some people have very rigid boundaries; they know when these have been broken and quickly seek to rectify the situation, often defensively and sometimes aggressively. For other people, their boundaries are rather flimsy and they can find themselves saying *"yes"* to things they do not want or being overly concerned about how others are feeling or what they think. The best boundaries are those that create space for you to be in touch with your inner self, so that you can know what is important to you plus what you want and how you want it. It gives you time to check in with yourself before you respond or react. But these boundaries also have flexibility. After you have reflected on your own values, you are able to consider the impact on others in a centred and grounded way. When we have effective boundaries, we interact more peacefully with the world.

8th September
Life's Irritants

Do you have irritants in your life? It may be particular frustrations like traffic jams or never-ending housework or it may be *that* person that just does *that* thing that drives you round the bend! But those aspects of life that irritate us are always opportunities for personal growth. We may be feeling like our buttons are being pushed but they are always our buttons to be pushed. So we have a choice, we can blame that person or thing for annoying us, or we can make peace with the situation and find a new way of being. It is never about the other person or thing, it is about the meaning we make of it. A traffic queue can be a troublesome delay, or it can be an opportunity for some inner reflection. That person's behaviour can be totally aggravating or it can be an opportunity to practice unconditional love and, of course, we will get the most benefit from that.

9th September
Self-love

Today is a good day to practice self-love. When your inner critic wants to berate you for a mistake you have made or something you probably should have done but haven't, it is time to be gentle and forgive yourself. Maybe you do want to do things differently in the future but blaming yourself is not going to inspire you to be different. Instead, when we are over-critical of ourselves, we are much more likely to repeat those behaviours or to find ourselves reaching for the nearest comfort item—that *naughty* treat, a glass or two of wine, or mindless TV watching, for example. When you are taking care of yourself, gently reassuring your critic that you are always good enough and encouraging yourself to reach for your dreams, our systems are flooded with feel-good hormones that make everything seem possible. Love yourself a little bit more today!

10th September
Your Life Commentator

Have you ever noticed that you have an internal chatterbox? This is the voice of your inner life commentator. At the subconscious level, our life commentator is continually analysing situations and drawing conclusions that can have an immense impact on our whole life. It is great when these comments uplift and inspire, yet when these judgments are less than helpful, we fall into the trap of believing them to be true and they become self-fulfilling in nature. Start to notice any of the throwaway comments you hear: "*life is a struggle*", "*I have to work hard*", "*no pain, no gain*". Is this something you really want to believe? Invite your life commentator to view the world differently by affirming: "*I am in my flow*", "*life is simple*", "*everything I want just seems to come to me effortlessly*" and watch how fast things begin to turn around.

11th September
Success

When you listen to the stories of successful people, it is interesting to spot themes and patterns that often go unnoticed. Ask someone at the pinnacle of their career about the secrets to their success and they will refer to the hard work and long hours they have put in to get to where they are today. But if you listen closely, you may hear a throwaway remark about a lucky break they got—a time when they just happened to be in the right place at the right time and a wonderful opportunity came their way. So is it pure coincidence that every successful person has had these moments of perfect synchronicity? Is it simply down to efforting or is there perhaps something else going on? What successful people also have in common is a compelling vision of what they want and the ability to use focus to move forwards confidently in that direction. When setbacks happen, they just reorientate themselves back towards their dreams. The Universe orchestrates life to arrange your meeting with miracles. You can continue to work hard and attribute your success to your effort or just let go of the struggle and allow the Universe to bring you what you want.

12th September
Your Life's Work

Do you enjoy your job? Does it leave you feeling satisfied and fulfilled or is it just the thing you do to pay the bills? You know when you have found the work that you were born to do when it no longer feels like work. When every day feels easy and effortless, you are contributing in a way that doesn't just serve others, it serves you. Being in alignment with our work is essential for living an inspired life. When it feels like efforting or a struggle, it depletes our energy levels and can lead to disease over the long term. Each of us has a unique talent and skill. We all have an area of expertise that can make a difference in the lives of others. Line up with your life purpose and take action today to share your gifts with the world.

13th September
Inherently Good

Each and every person in the world is fundamentally good. We are born that way. Over the years, our experiences shape who we are and it is that conditioning that generates our behaviour. Obviously not everyone is blessed to receive an inspiring and supportive upbringing and hence we occasionally hear or read stories that are shocking and upsetting. It is at these times that we need to dig deep and remember all of the good things about humanity. The majority of people want to make a difference and a real contribution in the world. The positives far outweigh the negatives. Let's look beyond the conditioning and believe in all that is good again. That way we get to be the uplifters and a force for optimism in the world.

14th September
Damage Limitation

When life deals us a blow, we are often quick to begin the damage limitation process. That is, we start to seek out how we can fix and solve things in our external world to rectify the problem. But if we move too soon to try to change our outer life, we can make the situation a great deal worse. Instead, pausing for a breath or two connects you to your own emotional state. What are the repairs you need to do on the inside? Do you need to forgive someone or even yourself for making a mistake? Do you need to heal your own wounds? What does your mind, body and spirit want for you in this moment? When we nurture our inner world first, it is actually the fastest route for solving any problem. Before you take action, remember that there is never anything more important than that you feel good.

15th September
Enthusiasm

How often do you feel enthusiastic? You only need to watch small children playing excitedly to know that enthusiasm is a naturally occurring state of being. Enthusiasm means *"the God (entheo) inside (ism)"*. When you experience enthusiasm, it is a reminder that we are all aspects of Divine spirit. Yet, sometimes, complications of daily life get in the way of our passion and excitement for life. So today the instruction from the JoyScope is to allow yourself to get truly, completely, head-over-heels giddy with enthusiasm for something in your life. The object of your passion could be anything—a hobby, a project, a person or even just a love of life in general. Light up your soul with pure enthusiasm and let the good times roll.

16th September
Playing with the Universe

Today is all about having fun! Sometimes, in the busy humdrum of life, we forget that we are here to have a good time. We can take ourselves a little too seriously rather than enjoying all of the fun that is waiting to be had. So why not lighten up? Even when all is not going to plan, find reasons to laugh with yourself and see the funny side of situations.

The Universe loves to play and as you let go of the need to try and control life and simply enjoy it instead, you will find yourself experiencing frequent moments of unexpected playfulness where you feel compelled to spread smiles and happiness everywhere you go. The best fun you can ever have is when you allow the Universe to play with you!

17th September
Cycles of Growth

Like all of nature, our lives progress in cycles of growth. It's good to notice the phases we are in so that we can adapt our approach and enhance the quality of our lives. Maybe you are in an active phase right now with lots of energy and creativity for new things. Or perhaps you are in a completion and rejuvenation phase when it is time to stop and rest, to allow the cycle to complete naturally, knowing that something new will grow from this stage in time. When we compete with our cycles, either by pushing on when our body and mind wants to be still or by not taking action when our inner guidance nudges us to start something new, we lose alignment with the core of our being. So the message today is to simply acknowledge and honour your natural cycles. Enjoy and appreciate every phase of growth because it is all completely essential for life.

18th September
All or Nothing

When we create goals in our life as being all or nothing, we tend to set ourselves up for failure. Patterns of thinking that are conditional on a certain result are doomed to failure. (For example, I must get *that* job, I must lose weight by *that* date, I must earn *that* amount of money this month). If the only way you can experience true happiness is when you have achieved your goal, you miss all of the pleasure of working and moving towards what you want. Instead, today, try making choices that allow for wriggle room and quick wins. (For example, "*I will send my CV speculatively to a company I have always wanted to work for*", "*I will walk to work instead of driving*", "*I will put an extra £10 in my saving account*"). Small actions culminate in really big results *and* allow you to have so much fun along the way. What will be the next small action you take today?

19th September
5 Positive P's

What P's are the cornerstones to living an inspired life?

Passion... the juice of life that keeps you in the flow.

Productivity... taking care of your needs (physical, emotional, spiritual and psychological well-being) so that you can perform and achieve the best quality of life.

Patience... the ability to allow and trust that everything happens at the perfect time, without forcing or trying to make things happen.

Perseverance... a willingness to stay committed to your dream, long after others would quit—It's never crowded along the extra mile!

Peace of Mind... No matter what is occurring in your external world, you still have that quiet, still, soulful place within that can observe your life without criticism or judgment.

Can you find new ways of cultivating more of these in your life?

20th September
Hidden Gifts

In any situation there is always a gift. Even the most difficult and challenging circumstances will have hidden benefits. When things aren't going according to plan, if we can stay centred and open, we have the opportunity to unlock even more resources. Every problem has the perfect solution. As soon as we become aware of the issue, we have also activated the resolution. It already exists. Our job is to clear our own resistance and blocks to allow the solution to find us. And the good news is that the end result tends to be a vast improvement on what we had before, plus we have learned and discovered more about who we are along the way. So today relax in the knowing that you can solve everything. It can be a lot easier that you think!

21st September
All That You Are

Today the message from JoyScope is to take a moment to reflect on who you have become. When you were younger you will have had hopes and dreams for how your life would turn out, maybe you even formed an identity of the kind of person you would be. So how are you measuring up to that? For some, you may be finding that life is exceeding your expectations yet for other people it may seem like you took a wrong turn somewhere along the path. Either way, know that it is always working out perfectly. Every experience you have, every challenge you face, and every decision you make is creating the version of you that is perfectly placed to have exactly the kind of life you would choose. When we trust the unfolding of life, we allow the opportunities to find us. So, as you reflect on your journey, make time to appreciate all that you have learnt and all that you have become and remind yourself of your own magnificence.

22nd September
Your Real Self at Work

Today is *take your whole self to work* day. Often our job roles have certain requirements for us to act and think in a certain way. There are a number of competencies that we are expected to demonstrate. But some of our greatest strengths are not always successfully deployed. And when we don't use these skills and talents, they begin to wither and the power of them declines. Today identify what qualities you have that are under-utilised at work. Make a deliberate choice to put them into play. It may be creativity or humour or logic or passion. What are your key strengths? Find outlets for the expression of these qualities and enjoy the thrill of being all of your authentic and real self at work. You may just surprise a few people!

23rd September
End of the World

There are many changes taking place in the Western world right now. Financial, environmental and cultural shifts are extensive and very rapid. We may hear rumours about the end of the world but this simply means the end of the world as we know it. Shifts and breakdowns are not necessarily bad. Often what emerges from the ashes is something even better. If we want to thrive over the next few years, we also need to adapt our thinking and attitude to the world. We are masters of our own destiny. We have more choice and more power to create our dreams, we only need absolute clarity about what we want. Today the JoyScope invites you to connect to your passion and purpose. What exciting things does the next phase of your life hold in store? Dream it, live it, love it and it will be!

24th September
Happy Without Reason

What would happen if you just decided to be happy today? No matter what is happening in your external environment, you can choose happiness. When you take a moment to bring your awareness into now and just be present, notice how all of the fears about the future and regrets about the past just seem to disappear. Is there anything else you *really* need right now? Or can you just be in this moment and appreciate all that you do have and allow the happiness to bubble up? When we find happiness without reason or justification, we give ourselves the greatest gift of life. When happiness is our residing state just because it is, nothing and no one can take it away.

25th September
Give It a Rest!

The message from the JoyScope today is to *give it a rest*! Our bodies and minds work hard for us and we tend not to give them the opportunities to rejuvenate that they deserve (and require). Today carve out moments to quieten the mind and allow the body to be still. Nurture yourself with quality rest periods and notice what a difference it can make. As we send the message to our body and mind that we are taking good care of ourselves, the response is new energy, new ideas, and a new overall sense of well-being.

26th September
Contribution

You will have heard the expression "*What goes around, comes around*". Although it is not always used in the most positive way, the statement is actually extremely valid. For whatever we give out to the world will eventually be returned. So the message today is to really consider what you want to be putting out there. Want more love in your life and/or the world? Then give more love. More happiness? Then give more happiness. More abundance? Then be abundant with whatever you have, even if it is simply sharing your time. Your gifts to others will not only be your contribution to the world but will enhance your life too.

27th September
Lessons from Children

Ever noticed how small children have an immense capacity for playing, finding games to play with simple and random objects that they find? Like the classic story of the child who receives an expensive Christmas toy and takes far more pleasure in playing with the box it came in. We all have an inner child that likes to play. It doesn't need designer gifts or the latest technology to have fun. It enjoys running in fields, playing with sand on the beach or indulging in water fights. What mischief would your inner child like to get up to today? Take a play break and have some fun connecting with your younger self.

28th September
Appreciation

Appreciation is the order of the day! Appreciation is a powerful quality because not only does it bring you into alignment with all that is but also it sends a message to the Universe asking for more of the same. Notice one thing (as least) that you can appreciate right now, in this very moment. It could be a special person or animal, an object of delight or desire, or simply the beauty of nature that surrounds us every day. As you stand in appreciation, notice what happens around you. As we appreciate the world, it reflects back on us.

29th September
Downtime

When lives are busy or we have been working intensively on projects or study, it is natural to feel as though we need to have some *downtime*. But the quality of our downtime can have a big impact on how quickly we feel refreshed and rejuvenated. We know what is naturally good for us—healthy food, exercise and sufficient sleep are necessary for a revitalized body. But we also need downtime for the mind. We may think we are recharging when we are watching TV or surfing the Internet or playing video games, yet our brains are still being bombarded with overloading activity. Instead, find ways to switch off. Sometimes just sitting in a quiet zone with the absence of any external stimulation can give your mind a restful break. When we commit to giving ourselves the very best in downtime, we maximise our energy and zest for life in the up-times.

30th September
Breathing

When we are continually stressed or on high alert, adrenalin floods our bodies and causes the natural biorhythms to change. That is why we experience disease and illness after long periods of stress and burnout. One of the simplest ways to begin to restore order in our systems is to practice breathing. Our culture tends to favour rapid response and action and hence our bodies are getting used to short, shallow breaths (known as the fire-breath in martial arts).

Today begin to reverse that process by taking big, deep, into-the-belly breaths. Try breathing in such a way that your exhale is twice as long as your inhale. This is just one way of activating the relaxation response and your body will love it. Happy body equals happy mind equals happy spirit!

1st October
Check-in (3)

So we are into the final quarter of this year. How has your year been? Have you managed to achieve what you want? If not, it is never too late to have an amazing year. When we start a new year, we tend to begin in a flurry of excitement and optimism that can sometimes disappear if we don't get the results we want as fast as we would like. But why wait until the next New Year to set your intentions and clarify your dreams? Why not simply begin now? By focusing on the next steps in your life now, by January 1st you will have such momentum and energy flowing that there will be no stopping you! What would need to happen in the next three months to make this your best year yet?

2nd October
Compliments

The JoyScope is setting you a challenge to be generous with your compliments. Today find as many people as you can to shower with appreciation and gratitude. Complimenting others is a great way to bring yourself into alignment, and it has a hugely positive effect on all those around you. Your feedback needs to be real and authentic. Try and stretch yourself—instead of commenting on their *nice hair*, find words to express the true essence of who they are. For example, *"I am so happy that I get to spend time with you, I always feel genuinely uplifted and inspired after our conversations"* will have a far greater impact. See how many people you can touch with your words today!

3rd October
Forgive Yourself

From time to time, we all make mistakes or behave in ways that aren't in alignment with who we really are. It's all part of being human. We came to live our lives fully, not to seek perfection. Hindsight is wonderful but we must remember that we are always doing the best that we can in the moment. We are often more forgiving to other people than to ourselves. So is there something that you need to forgive yourself for? When we let ourselves off the hook, we free up valuable energy for living an expansive and wonderful life. Forgive, forget and love yourself today!

4th October
Inspiration List

We are meant to live with inspiration. Its the passion and enthusiasm of being alive and knowing that we have endless opportunities to create, to play, to love, to laugh, and to be free. When we are feeling less than uplifted, the only action we *need* to take is the journey towards inspiration. So what inspires you? A chat with a friend or your partner, a walk in nature, some quiet solitude, an inspiring book or movie—you get to choose. Create a list of inspirations—simple activities that bring you back into alignment and refer to it whenever you are in need of a *hit*! When we live from a place of inspiration, we live through joy.

5th October
Who Cares?

Do you ever come across people who never seem to appreciate you? It can seem like no matter what you do, it's never enough. You can't do right for doing wrong! Have you ever tried to convince them of your worth? Tried pointing out all your efforts to little or no avail? How well has that been working for you? It's so easy to get caught in the mindset that they *should* appreciate you and to feel indignant and hurt that they don't care. But the truth is that it isn't their job to appreciate you—it's yours! It also isn't their job to care about you—it's yours. Of course, recognition and appreciation always feels nice but when we focus on the absence of it, we are just hurting ourselves. Instead, find the joy in simply helping them because that is who you are, and let go of the need for approval and gratitude. When you let them off the hook, you are really freeing yourself to feel good!

6th October
Releasing Victimhood

You are a powerful creator. It can be a little too easy to forget that sometimes. When we are not remembering who we really are, we can slip into *victim* type thoughts about the things that are happening *to* us. But when we are in touch with the magnificence of our true selves, we remember that at some level, albeit unconsciously, we have asked for that situation. Every experience brings a gift— sometimes we get what we want, sometimes we get an opportunity to learn and make finer distinctions about our dreams and desires. So *either* way is better. Step back into your power today and enjoy the thrill of being the powerful creator of your life.

7th October
Life Analogy

Do you have an analogy for life? Do you think of life as being like a journey or an uphill struggle or a playground? The story we tell ourselves about how easy or difficult life can be has a powerful impact on the quality of our experiences. You get to choose your metaphor. Try writing down your responses to the statement *"Life is..."*. If any of these are less than positive, turn them around to find a more empowering description. What we believe about life we will live out—*all ways*!

8th October
Smiling

Today is a very good day for smiling. It really doesn't matter whether you are smiling on the outside or, if you would prefer, you can be sneakily grinning on the inside—the key thing is to find a reason to smile. And there is always a reason. Even in the darkest moments you may discover your mind drifting off and settling on thoughts of a loved one, a powerful and uplifting memory or maybe just a really good joke you once heard. Of course the benefit of smiling on the outside is that it tends to be contagious and you may just find people inanely grinning back at you—it just becomes a vicious smile circle you can't escape from! I'm smiling at you now. Are you smiling back?

9th October
Natural Seasons

As the nights begin to draw in, it is worth remembering that we too have our natural seasons. There are times of new ideas flourishing like spring, times of rapid growth like summer, times of harvesting like autumn, and times of reflection and renewal when things lie more dormant just like winter. Today just take note of your own natural season. Are you feeling more reflective or more inspired? Do you need more re-charge time or are you bursting with ideas that you need to pursue? Follow your energy and allow the natural cycles and notice how much more you are able to achieve.

10th October
Daydreaming

The message from the JoyScope today is to allow your mind to wander free. When our lives are packed with *shoulds* and *oughts* and *musts*, we stifle our creativity and passion. At school we are taught that daydreaming is a worthless occupation; that we can learn more from books than we can from the thoughts and musings of our mind. Yet to really learn our truth, we need time and space to be able to listen and hear our inner voice. If you simply allow fifteen minutes of pure, uninhibited, totally indulgent day-dreaming a day, this inner wisdom will dramatically increase. And you may just get to be delightfully surprised by the ideas and inspirations that follow. Free your mind to wander today!

11th October
Your Unique Perspective

Each of us has a unique perspective on life. No one else has had exactly the same experiences. No one else has exactly the same values and beliefs. No one else has lived the way that we have lived. When we reflect on all the learning and wisdom we have accumulated, we each have a special message to share with the world. Maybe it is an understanding of parenting, relationships or leadership. Maybe we have discovered a way to keep fit or stay in shape or eat for energy. Maybe we know how to be at one with nature or to entertain or simply to be in the flow of life. When you share your message and use your talents to help others, you inspire and uplift people around you. And that makes the world a better place to be. So what aspects of yourself can you share to uplift others today?

12th October
Appreciating Miracles

Do you celebrate your miracles in life? We are surrounded by magic every day, yet we don't always take time to acknowledge and appreciate them. Short of ideas? Just look to the natural world. What about the fact that the earth spins around the sun every three hundred and sixty five and a quarter days? I'm sure nature threw in that last quarter just for fun! What about water? It is composed of two different elements naturally occurring as gases that combine to form a liquid that life depends upon. Or trees? Take a huge oak tree that has probably existed for hundreds of years. Imagine what it has witnessed and the stories of life it could tell. And what about you? Isn't it a miracle that you are here—a mass of energy that vibrates at such a high frequency that you appear to have a physical form? You are the biggest miracle in your life. So go on, take a big bow and hear the applause.

13th October
Technological Advances

We live in a land of opportunity. With all of the technological advances over the last century, life is supposed to be so much easier. We have machines to wash our clothes and dishes, we can bulk buy fresh food and keep it chilled, we can send mail to people at the push of a button and we can travel from A to B incredibly fast—even when B is the other side of the world! Yet rather than using these services to enhance our life, too often we allow them to dominate our lives. So the message today is to develop awareness of when we are being controlled by technology rather than the other way around. It is far too easy to become responsive to the demands of technology to the detriment of your inner peace. Remember the gift that these opportunities present in our lives and use them wisely.

14th October
Open Your Eyes!

Our lives consist of the multitude of perceptions and judgments we are making of the world. But they are limited to what we are capable of seeing. There is a story that when Christopher Columbus approached America, the natives couldn't see the ships. It was only when a Shaman noticed the ripples on the water that he was able to make out shapes on the horizon. Because they had no reference experiences for a ship, they literally couldn't perceive them. So in how many ways are we deleting important information from our experiences? What is there that you haven't yet seen? Open your eyes and your heart. It's time to make the invisible visible!

15th October
Trust and Then Trust Some More!

When we are aligning ourselves behind a particular desire, it can be less than easy to believe it is going to happen in the absence of any real evidence. This can lead us to lose focus on what we want and so our attention is drawn to what we have not yet got. For example, you want the inspired relationship but your life demonstrates that you are still single or you want financial abundance but your bank account still reflects the lack of cash flow. Whatever you want is on its way so long as you stay focused in the right direction. Trust, trust, trust and then trust some more! When you believe, it is not only possible, it is totally inevitable!

16th October
Clock Watching

Much of our life is governed by clocks—at work we clock-watch for that time when we can clock off. Women who want children often find that their biological clock starts ticking at a certain age. Even in our every day language we talk about being up against the clock when we have too much to do in too little time. What we are forgetting is that time is a man-made construct. In our quest to label life experience, we have even taken natural cycles and forced them to conform to our structures, from centuries and decades right down to minutes and seconds. And so our lives are dictated by these external measurements rather than the natural flow of our lives. So today, for as long or as little as you can manage, let go of the need to clock watch and tune into your natural rhythms instead. Move when you are inspired to move and rest when you are guided to rest. Find ways to come back into your natural cycle and you may be surprised by how much ease you bring to your life.

17th October
Get Moving

Our bodies love to move. The human body is not designed for sitting but for being active and getting around. Our ancestors used their bodies much more effectively in hunting and foraging for food. We don't quite get the same effect when walking around a supermarket! We spend too much time cooped up in homes and offices and cars. It's time to get moving. So tap into your body wisdom today. How would it like to move? Maybe a walk in a forest or some vigorous exercise or perhaps just a good old boogie? Today have fun moving your body. It will thank you for the workout.

18th October
Inner Guru

When you need good advice, whom do you turn to? Do you have supportive and life-affirming friends who hold your best interests at heart? Do you have a coach or mentor that can help you to make sense of difficult situations or challenges? Do you have a partner who knows you intimately and always finds a way to say exactly the right thing at the right time? Well maybe you do and maybe you don't have one or more of these but what you definitely have is an inner guru. Your inner guru is perfectly placed to point you in the right direction or offer a helping hand. It is the wiser, all-knowing, infinite part of you and it is always present and always listening. Can you say the same thing? We tend to get caught up in our world of thoughts and business and forget to pay attention to the messages from our soul. So today take time to tune in and take note. After all, your inner guru is the only one that has lived every experience with you!

19th October
Living is Learning

We are presented with so many opportunities to learn in life. Sometimes we instantly have an a-ha moment when everything falls into place; sometimes it takes a little bit longer. Either way is perfect! When we beat ourselves up for not getting it first time, we actually drag out the process even more. The learning may be complex or require further and finer distinctions in order for us to really know the truth. Rest assured, if it is important for our personal growth, we will be presented with more opportunities to expand our understanding. Be gentle with yourself and enjoy the knowledge that just by living you are learning.

20th October
Your Super-computer

We have access to our very own super-computer! Our wonderful minds have an incredible capacity for handling complex tasks and retaining vast amounts of data. Just consider all of the functions that are handled outside our conscious control. For example, regulating our bodies and handling day-to-day processes so that we can walk, drive and talk without expending too much energy. But new activities do consume more brainpower. Before we can automate something, we need to give it more conscious attention. That is why, when we change jobs, begin a different routine or learn a new activity, it can be more tiring. And, just as a computer with many programmes running starts to slow and under-perform, if we try to take on too much at once, the result is stress and eventual burnout. So the message from the JoyScope today is to give you space to think. Rather than attempting to multi-task, just focus on the main thing in the moment. Your super-computer will find optimal performance when you close down the unnecessary files.

21st October
Driving Hard

We often find ourselves working way too hard for what we want. When we are feeling in the flow, things happen naturally and effortlessly. What we want seems to just *show up* at the right time and the right place. If you are not experiencing enough flow in your life, rather than driving harder for what you want, take some space and quiet time to reconnect to what is most important—your peace of mind and wellbeing. So today take a time out to meditate, walk or simply practice deep breathing. When we are lined up with what we want rather than resisting what is, we allow all the good things to come in.

22nd October
Aloneness

Are you willing to be alone? It may seem like a strange question but many of us spend too much of our time surrounded by the noise and distraction of our external environment. And some of us often resist spending time alone because we equate aloneness with loneliness. But aloneness has a very different quality. It is a willingness to take a deliberate step back from external stimuli and to spend time connecting to the still small voice within. Our inner guidance is the source of our creativity, inspiration and peace of mind. So whether you are retreating from the hustle and bustle of everyday life or simply embracing the quiet time you experience on your own, give yourself the gift of some *alone* time today.

23rd October
Cut the Rope

Far too often, the limitations we have in life are simply perceived obstacles that don't truly exist in reality. There is a story about a baby elephant that is tied to a tree with a piece of rope, only able to wander the distance of the length of the rope. As the elephant grows, his power and strength far exceeds the rope (and probably the tree) yet because he has spent his life only able to stray a small distance, he doesn't even try to move further and so break the rope. In a similar way, we internalise feedback from well-meaning people in the early part of our lives about what we are and what we are not capable of and, like the elephant, we give up trying to be anything different. So the message today is that it is time to cut the rope. You have limitless potential waiting to be explored. Move beyond your limitations!

24th October
Doubt the Doubt

Perhaps the fastest way to undermine our self-confidence is to let doubt creep in. So the message from the JoyScope today is simple—*doubt the doub*t! So many times we have an idea or inspiration to do something and it's just our limiting beliefs that hold us back. What would you do if you knew you couldn't fail and success was the *only* option? You are good enough. You deserve happiness. You are worthy of all of your desires. Take time now to reassure that doubting part of you that all is well and will continue to be well. Trust instead the voice of your inner cheerleader who supports and encourages you every step of the way and reminds you daily of your magnificence.

25ᵗʰ October
Acknowledgment

We have probably all had the experience of feeling a lack of appreciation for who we are or what we do. Life is moving so fast that is practically impossible to keep up with it all. Special occasions get missed, our achievements may go unnoticed or our greatest contributions fall through the gaps and remain unacknowledged. This gives us a choice. Do we mope and moan that our efforts have been in vain or do we shift our mindset and decide to perceive it all differently? It's good to ask ourselves what it has all really been for. Do you do the things you do because of the acknowledgments they bring or rather do you do what you do because it is fundamentally who you are? When we remind ourselves that giving generously of our time, energy and love is more about who we are at the core of our being, we stop demanding others to meet our needs for validation. Appreciation becomes the cherry on top. A nice decoration but certainly not a requirement for a tasty bite!

26ᵗʰ October
Stillness

Today you are invited to find your inner stillness. We all have a part that is able to drop silently into the now and just be fully present to our inner world. Even when the outer world is chaotic and demanding, the quiet place within is always available. Just as the centre of a tornado always remains completely calm, we can be surrounded by whirlwinds and yet remain effortlessly connected to that peaceful and tranquil place inside us. Take time today to just sit and be still. Notice your inner world and remember times in your life when you have felt pure relaxation. Gradually let go of any racing thoughts to allow yourself to feel truly at ease. Just five minutes a day can help you to stay calm and centred, even when the rest of life has its crazy moments.

27th October
Leaving a Legacy

If you had one top tip to share with the world to make it a better place, what would it be? Everyone possesses wisdom but our individual experiences means that there may be something you have learnt along the journey of life that other people might not know. Think of some of the greatest quotations you have heard like *"A journey of a thousand miles begins with a single step"* – Lao-Tzu or *"It's time to start living the life you've imagined"* - Henry James. These powerful phrases transport people to a higher level of consciousness and awareness. Imagine that you were leaving a legacy. What would you say?

28th October
A Little Bit Weird

There is so much more information available to us these days that we often complicate life by trying to live up to cultural standards or images portrayed by the media. The truth is that you only ever need to live up to your heart's desire. Let go of any expectations of how you should or shouldn't be. Choose what is applicable for you and forget the rest. There is no need for you to conform to a fantasy projection. You only end up wasting valuable energy trying to squeeze yourself into a box that will ultimately hold you back. Break the norms, stand out and be different. Being a little bit weird can have some real advantages!

29th October
Energy

Some people just seem to have boundless energy. They live life to the max and exude vibrancy and vitality. Are you one of these people? If not, would you like to be? Well it may be a lot easier than we are led to believe. Yes, the essential components of a healthy lifestyle, nutritious diet and sufficient sleep are important but energy really flows when we are feeling aligned with an absolute desire for life. Don't you find you have surges of energy when you know you have something exciting planned, like a holiday or a celebration? Children never have trouble getting out of bed on birthdays and at Christmas! So today find more ways to do things that you are passionate about. When we do what we love, our energy knows no limits!

30th October
Beyond Approval-seeking

Do you find that you care too much about the opinion of others? Do you worry about what they may think about you, whether you are getting it right or what they say behind your back? Have you ever stopped to consider why? In all honesty, does their view of you really matter? We get caught up in concerning ourselves with others' opinions because we want to be cared about. And as terrible as it often feels, approval seeking is a way of knowing whether or not they care. We mistakenly believe that if people care, we won't ever find ourselves alone. The trouble is that when they hold a negative judgment, we are still getting that need met and so we get wrapped up in their opinion and it becomes all encompassing. We lose ourselves in their perception and the truth of the situation eludes us. Instead, just find relief in the knowledge that you will never be alone as long as you are connected to the inner you. To find peace, make that relationship the most important in your life and create the space to listen to the gentle and soothing words from your soul.

31st October
Happy Halloween!

Happy Halloween! At this time of year, children and parents play games with ghosts and ghouls and reveling in all things spooky. Everyone knows these things are made up for fun. Yet when it comes to our fears, which are usually completely unfounded, we seem to forget that we are making up that story too. So today have fun with Halloween and stop terrifying yourself with things that may or may not happen. Let go of the stress and anxiety of what the future will bring and just focus on all the good things that are in your life right now. There are sure to be some treats lined up for you!

1st November
Speak from the Heart

The art of powerful communication is to speak from the heart. Even the most difficult conversations can be transformed when we authentically share the truth of who we are and what we are feeling. When we realise we are all doing the best that we can in the moment, there is never a need to shame or blame. Trust that no one would intentionally hurt or offend another person. Take ownership of your reactions and allow the wisest part of you to be your guide. Today create the space for the people around you to freely be themselves. As you do, you will open your heart to connection on a whole new level.

2nd November
Your Life Story

Today the message from the JoyScope is to tell your life story! It is often said that we all have a book within us but most of us will never put pen to paper to share our message. You may not be the next Catherine Cookson or Frederick Forsyth but you don't need to be a best-selling author to have a story to tell. Think about all the wisdom you have gained over the years through the many experiences you have had, the mistakes you have made and the knowledge you have learnt. Don't you think that there may be at least one person who could benefit immensely from what you have to offer? This isn't about securing a publishing deal or getting an Amazon best seller. Even a handwritten journal could end up being your greatest gift to your children, your children's children, or your friends and family. Having your story in print (or handwritten) allows you to leave your legacy when you eventually transition and the best of who you are will continue to live on.

3rd November
Empowerment

When we are born we are helpless and powerless. Our very existence depends on those around us. It is hardly surprising that we give away our power to other people—it is the basis of our survival. As we grow and mature, we come to realise our capability and we gradually free ourselves from that dependence on others. Unfortunately, often for very good reasons our evolution doesn't quite happen as expected and we find that we continue to give away our power beyond any necessity or use it may have. In fact, it may be extremely detrimental to the quality of our life. Today the JoyScope wants to empower you. Reflect on the areas of your world where you continue to play it small or give yourself away to others. Remember that it is your life and only your life and so the power always lies with you.

4th November
Lifestyle

Does your lifestyle support your dreams? Many of us long for more quality time with our family and loved ones, space and freedom for self-expression, more energy and vitality to pursue our interests or time to travel and see the world. Yet we spend our time on less than fulfilling pursuits—stuck working 9-5 in an unsatisfying job, doing chores or other activities out of a sense of obligation or meaningless distractions such as watching TV or mindlessly surfing the internet. So the invitation from the JoyScope today is to get present to your life. Make decisions on what you give your time and attention to consciously and with intent. Remember that everything happening in our life today was once a choice and we can always choose differently. It's your life. Make it count!

5th November
Bonfire Night

Tonight is bonfire night here in the UK and as the skies darken there will be no escaping the sounds and sights of firework displays. It is somewhat interesting to note that this custom began as a result of the failed Gunpowder Plot of 1605 but celebrating bonfire night has become a tradition that looks set to stay. However, there are many historical events that have been much more inspiring and uplifting in nature. When you consider all of these, which one particularly stands out for you and why? Often when we resonate with a certain event it is because the situation required certain qualities or strengths to be successful. For example, think of the passion and conviction of Martin Luther King delivering his "*I have a dream*" speech in 1963. We admire these qualities because they also exist within us, although often suppressed. So as we celebrate bonfire night today, think of the event you would truly like to celebrate and as the fireworks light up the sky remember all of those amazing qualities that you possess.

6th November
Uninsurable Fear

We live in a world that fears loss. We insure our possessions and back-up our data as a safety measure to save us from the worst-case scenario. But even with the best possible risk-avoidance strategies, our dreaded worst fears may still happen. There is simply never going to be enough insurance to protect us from all of life's mishaps. There are two ways of looking at this. We can worry and fret about what might happen or we can make a conscious decision that we will instead trust our ability to handle whatever life presents. The best insurance we can ever experience is the kind that lives on the inside. It comes from just knowing that all will be well—if not right now, very soon. Computers and files will sometimes crash. Luggage and belongings will sometimes disappear. Loss will occasionally happen. Yet the feeling of security will always be there when it lives on the inside.

7th November
Rightness

Have you ever found yourself in a somewhat heated discussion with someone who refused to back down? Did you absolutely know you were right but their response was to stonewall or argue back for their rightness? Did you continue to present evidence, develop your argument and demonstrate how right you were in an attempt to influence them to take on your point of view? How well did that work out for you? I'm guessing the answer is probably *not so well*!

When we attempt to highlight how wrong someone is in a situation, we only pour petrol on the fire of their argument and strengthen their conviction in what they are saying. Couldn't the same be said of you? When someone points out that you are wrong, doesn't your determination make you feel even more right? So here is today's question: *In the grand scheme of things, does it really matter who is right and who is wrong?* Sometimes there just comes a point when you want to shake hands and agree to disagree. The message from the JoyScope today is to pick your battles carefully. It's worth considering—do you want to be right or do you want to be happy?

8th November
Life is a Movie

If your life was a movie, which one would it be? Consider the types of movie that you most resonate with—a drama, an action thriller, a romantic comedy, a fairytale, or an epic? It can be interesting to discover the unconscious script we are writing for our lives. When we are living to a certain *blueprint*, we will be fulfilling the spec, often without realising it! But the good news is that you can change your story today, in whatever way you want. If you could have a different movie, with different themes and a perhaps a different ending, what would it be? Become the director of your life and have fun creating your movie the way you want it to be.

9th November
Make Your Move

Is there something that you have been putting off? Maybe a decision or a change that you really know you should make but just can't seem to make the first move? When we view the world from our limited perspective, we aren't always aware of the wonderful benefits that come from taking a step into the unknown. So today the JoyScope is here to guide you. Beyond what you can currently perceive, wonderful things are lined up and waiting for you. There is no need to delay any further. Take the first step, knowing and trusting that the Universe will conspire to support you. What will unfold will be better than you could ever imagine. Why would you want to hold yourself back from all of that? It's all there for the taking—go on, make your move!

10th November
New Beliefs

Our beliefs are forms of automatic programming that repeatedly take us in a certain direction. Some of our beliefs can be empowering and supportive, but some are less than helpful and even limiting. But beliefs are just thoughts we keep thinking. If you imagine an overgrown and wild field, when we think a thought we cut through the growth. The first time it barely makes a difference. But if we tread the same ground over and over again, it is not long before we have carved out a path. Once the path is there, it becomes easier to stay on the same route than to change direction.

If your beliefs are limiting you, it's time to carve out a new path. It may take a small amount of effort at the beginning to change your thoughts but the benefits are huge! Change your thoughts and change your life. What do you want to believe about yourself today?

11th November
Treat Yourself

The JoyScope message today is that it's time to treat yourself. Treats sometimes get a bad press; that in some way we are more honourable and worthy when we deprive ourselves or act as a martyr. Nothing could be further from the truth. Is it really worth suffering our way through life for some mistaken credibility we think we will receive at the end? Life is here to be gloriously and deliciously enjoyed. So pick something today that feels indulgent and enjoy every minute of spoiling yourself. Whether it is booking a day off work to have some fun, investing your time in a hobby or being with friends, or maybe a massage or other treat, pick something that nourishes your soul and lifts your spirits and notice how good it feels. Enjoy treating yourself today!

12th November
Quantum Change

When you look at your current circumstances, perhaps there are one or more areas of life that you really want to change, yet just don't know where to start. Maybe you think that even if you knew where to start, the journey to what you want would be long and laborious? What if it didn't have to be that way? The truth is that there is nothing that cannot happen today! We tend to think in sequential next steps but when we truly line up with something that we want and allow it to come to us, change can happen in quantum leaps. Stop concerning yourself with how much time it may take and enjoy knowing that it is on its way.

13th November
Keep It Simple

Today the theme from the JoyScope is to *keep it simple*! When we are aligned with a particular decision or course of action, life will naturally flow with ease. Things only get complicated when we are running thoughts of uncertainty or doubt. So today practise doing the things that feel most easy. Take the next logical and simple step. If it feels overwhelming or frightening, it's too big or too complex. Just break it down into something more simple and straightforward. There is always an easier way of we are willing to look. So uncomplicate your life. As you do, you will notice how it conspires to bring you what you want!

14th November
Finding Your Flow

What happens when being in the flow eludes you? Do you gird your loins and grit your teeth and plow on regardless? If so, you will tend to find that life just gets harder and harder. There is only so much river pushing you can do before you wear yourself out! And once your strength has gone, there is nothing else for it but to succumb to the force of what is, give in and let a great tidal wave wash over you. But then an intriguing thing will happen. In the moment you let go and surrender to the very thing you were fighting against, things miraculously start to improve again. Interesting hey? We resist what is happening until we can take it no more, then let go and the flow of life finds us again. What if from the outset we simply gave up the fight and allowed the flow to take us instead? Just a thought!

15th November
Throw Down a Rope Ladder

Have you ever been in conversation with a friend, family member or colleague in despair and found yourself sliding right into that unresourceful place with them? We are told that good listening is to be sympathetic or empathic, which means putting ourselves in their shoes and experiencing the world just as they do. It may seem like you are being a good friend and it can be very validating for their issue but it is of no real use to moving them beyond their problem. Whilst it is great for gathering information about their situation, if the place they are in is less than uplifting, you will soon find your own energy and happiness rapidly diminishing. Instead of climbing in the pit with them, the best form of listening is when you are able to stand at the top of the pit, with total awareness of the struggle that they face but with the ability to throw a rope ladder down to them. Your willingness to stay outside the problem vastly increases your ability to be of service. So next time you are faced with a friend in need, throw down the rope ladder and gently support them in finding the way out.

16th November
Inaction

Today's JoyScope message is a gentle nudge to keep moving towards your dreams. Right now, in the Western world, there is a huge resistance to taking action. The intense uncertainty of not knowing what will happen over the next few months and years is causing us to put our greatest desires on hold. We are waiting for a change in the economic climate to give us the certainty to take action. But our life stagnates when we aren't moving forwards and that is of no benefit to anyone and is certainly not the recipe for a happy and fulfilling life. Even if you can't yet see the entire path to your dream destination, just take a step in the right direction. Life is too short to hold yourself back!

17th November
Wish List

What good feelings are on your wish list today—Happiness? Peace? Inspiration? Love? Bliss? Passion? What does your body, mind and soul desire? Nothing is ever more important than how we feel as the quality of our life experiences will always flow from the place we are in. So as you consider what juicy feelings you would like to have today, set an intention to spend more time focused on creating those emotional states. In fact, if you have a to-do list, whether written down or just held in your mind, consciously put the emotional state that you want at the top of the list! Add some small steps and actions that you can take that will create more of those feelings today. Make how you feel your biggest wish!

18th November
Self-advise

Our lives are down to us. It doesn't matter what anyone else thinks. We get to decide what is right for us. The opinions of others are simply their interpretation of events. No one else has lived your life or experienced your experiences. Therefore, no one is better placed to advise you than yourself. It can be useful to listen to what others say, but this is simply data gathering. They may help you to expand your perspective or to make a new distinction but the choice always rests with you. So what advice would you like to give to yourself today? What choices are right for you? What direction are you ready to take? Wonderful guidance can come from self-advice!

19th November
Love on the Inside

What is love? The general belief is that when we experience those feelings and sensations associated with love, it is down to the object of our affection. We talk of falling in love when we meet that special someone who matches our wishes and desires; someone who makes us feel good when we are in their presence; someone who behaves in a way that meets or even exceeds our expectations. In fact, falling in love is an inside job. It's not that we fall in love with the other person so much as that in focusing on their most positive attributes and qualities, we raise our own vibration and create the state of love inside ourselves. It's great to have an object of desire to flow our appreciation towards but if we make it all about the other person, our loving state is potentially jeopardised. What happens if that other person behaves in a way that is less than our expectations or worse still, withdraws their love altogether. Then our love is diminished or even disappears. If we remember that we fall in love not because of the other person but because of the story we are telling ourselves in that moment, our state of love is solidified. Love becomes a choice rather than dependent on anyone or anything—we can love openly once more.

20th November
Arguing with Reality

Do you ever find yourself wishing that something could be different to how it is? The problem with wishing things were different is that we put ourselves in a position of arguing with reality and that is a battle we are always going to lose! If there is a situation that can be changed, taking positive and aligned action is a really good thing. But if we can't find a way to change it, wishing it would be different is just going to drain our energy away. So next time you are feeling stuck, overwhelmed or despondent, ask yourself what reality you are battling against. Make peace with how things are and relax into knowing that everything works out perfectly over time.

21st November
The Focus Game

We will always get more of what we focus upon. Do you find yourself thinking about your unlimited potential or are you more often berating yourself for not doing a good enough job or getting it right? Today is all about ensuring that you are focused on your unique gifts and talents so that you can bring more of them to your life. So here is the challenge: Starting with the letter *A*, find a strength or skill that you have beginning with that letter. Work your way through the alphabet compiling an alphabetical list of your greatest assets (a little poetic licence is allowed with the letter *X*—maybe you are *eXcellent* or *eXceptional*!) Once you are done, read the list and notice how you feel. Playing this game might just put a spring in your step when you realise quite how magnificent you are.

22nd November
Reflection

The importance of quiet reflection time cannot be underestimated. Reflection is the path to building a solid relationship with your soul. But there are different ways to reflect. We can review our experiences with a critical eye searching for opportunities for self-improvement or we can gently seek out the times when we have surprised ourselves with our loving nature, our resourcefulness or our talent. The journey of personal growth is essential to living but when you are fixated on improving yourself, you never get to experience the absolute peace of knowing how wonderful you are right now, just as you are. When we choose to reflect on our most positive aspects, we get to bask in the joy of self-admiration. We will still evolve through knowing and loving ourselves better—and that is the kind of relationship our soul just loves to have.

23rd November
Relaxation

Ever find yourself in that pattern of thought that says, "*When I get all of this done, then I will relax*"? Ever have times when the point of relaxation never seems to appear? When we believe that relaxation is a reward for efforting and hard work, we actually set ourselves up for a never-ending cycle of struggle. That is because instead of bringing us peace and calmness, forcing ourselves to get things done just creates even more things that require our attention and time. If we know that we are the creators of our own reality, we know that the energy of what we are doing attracts more situations that are a vibrational match to our emotional state. Even if we are sceptical, there have probably been times that you can recall when you have tried to take rapid action to get something done and out of the way, only to find it snowballs into a much more complex or time-consuming task. For example, you decide to shoot off a quick email and your computer or the Internet crashes or you are preparing for guests and rushing to clean the house when the vacuum decides to blow out rather than suck up! So why wait for relaxation? Make that the number one priority in your life. It will make everything much easier in the long run.

24th November
Financial Awakening

It's easy in these times of economic doom and gloom to get hooked into a scarcity mentality. The media exacerbates the problem by over-emphasising the issue and continually feeding the drama of the financial crisis. In the face of such prolonged negative reporting, hanging on to our feelings of abundance can be a real challenge. If we follow the herd, we are likely to get swallowed up by the same thinking, namely that there is not enough to go around. No one is denying the financial upheavals in our current economic climate; it just doesn't serve us to be consumed by a scarcity mentality. There is always an unlimited supply of abundance that you can line yourself up with. Today take time to notice all the gifts that come to you, whether it is money, savings and discounts or purely synchronicities. We are abundant beings living in an abundant universe. The Universe wants to give you money!

25th November
Transitions

Life occasionally gets messy! It can seem as though we have hit a streak of misfortune. We have lots of expressions in our culture to explain these periods in our life—*"a run of bad luck"* or *"life is throwing us curve balls"* or *"problems come in threes!"* But there may be other reasons why we experience these tumultuous times that have a more positive connotation. During our lifetime we will go through many different cycles and between each cycle is a transition. Sometimes these transitions are small and insignificant but sometimes we reach a point when we have simply outgrown every aspect of our lives and it is time for a full reshuffle. The Universe always knows what we want and will help us to manifest it, as long as we stay in a place of non-resistance to what is happening. The fastest way through a transition is to give less attention to the problems and much more of your energy and resources to the vision of what you want instead.

26th November
Comparisons

We can make our lives so much harder than they need to be when we are comparing ourselves to everyone else. If we perceive that someone is doing more for us than we are for them, we feel guilty. If we think we are doing more for them than we get back in return, we can feel burdened or resentful. This makes our relationships more complicated than they need to be. So why not just make it simple? Give freely without any expectation of return. Do it for the pure joy of giving the best of you and let go of the need for acknowledgment or recognition. Let the good feelings of giving generously be your reward. And express gratitude for any good deeds directed your way because appreciation is the best return anyone could ever want. If we all lived our relationships from this perspective, conflict would diminish and our communities would be strengthened. Doesn't that just make more sense?

27th November
Refuel

When our cars get low on fuel, we automatically know that we should go and top up or the car will stop running. Sometimes we are less aware when it comes to ourselves and our bodies. So what does your fuel gauge say? Are you getting a little low on juice or even running on empty? If so, the message from JoyScope today is to go and re-fuel! Whether it is a lunchtime walk, a massage or even a day off, the benefits of quality time out are immense. With a full tank, we are much more able to have a smooth and uninterrupted journey through life!

28th November
Creative Intentions

It is a wonderful feeling when you set an intention and then get to watch it cycle through beginning, middle and end. There is something deeply satisfying and fulfilling about nurturing a project or creating a masterpiece. Whether that is an art project like a sculpture or oil painting, gardening or growing vegetables, learning a new language or writing a book—to take something from small beginnings to completion and fruition is deeply nourishing for the soul. So what project or masterpiece is calling to you? What new creation is ready to be born through you? You can make it as big or as small as you would like but make the process a joyful journey of discovery. Give yourself the gift of time to enjoy every step along the path so you can watch it unfold with awe and amazement. When we align our creative energy with the Universe, truly magical things can happen!

29th November
Anticipation

We all need a little something to look forward to! It's great to have a special occasion or a holiday scheduled in our diaries to keep our spirits high but it's even better to have something to joyfully anticipate each and every day! What are the little things that make your heart sing? Maybe some quality time with your family or friends, or a warm bubble bath, or curling up with a good book. Make a list of the things that you most like to anticipate. And any time you want a mood boost, you can simply look at your list and find inspiration in anticipation. What would you like to anticipate today?

30th November
Injunctions

We probably all like to think of ourselves as being happy and well-rounded individuals. To a large extent we are. Except that underneath the surface, we all have injunctions about what is and what it not acceptable. It may be that you don't think it is okay to ask for what you want and need but of course it absolutely is, just as it is absolutely okay for the other person to decline if they so wish. We may have injunctions that certain emotions are inappropriate or unacceptable and so we hide our anger with a false smile or hold back the tears when we hurt most. Or we may feel that we can't speak out or question authority figures, forgetting that our opinions are always equally valid. When we let go of these injunctions, we free ourselves to be authentic. And the world would be a happier and more content place if we all allowed ourselves to be real.

1st December
Check-in (4)

As we enter the last month of the year, it's a good time to start data gathering for next year's wish list. We really can have, be or do anything that we want. Anything can happen and everything is possible. Start dreaming your dreams for next year. What do you want to create? Dream big, dream huge, dream expansive—after all, it is *your* dream! Pick one thing that would enable you to end the year and say with pride "*I did that!*" Whether it is something small or a great big adventure, make the choice today to go for your dreams!

2nd December
Parental Role Models

Being a parent or a role model for children has the potential to bring immense joy into our lives yet it can be the most challenging role we will ever have. Finding a balance between setting boundaries and teaching life skills whilst being loving, supportive and allowing children to be themselves can sometimes be less than easy. Sometimes it can seem as though they won't listen to a word we say! There is a good reason for this. Our children will always respond more to who we are than what we say. When we are authentic and aligned, we offer a model that children can understand

and aspire to in their own way. Spending a little less of our energy trying to convince children to be a certain way and a little more time on our own inner relationship reaps big rewards.

3rd December
Stories

Worry, anxiety and concern are all bi-products of planning a future with fear. What will happen tomorrow is uncertain and even seemingly hopeless circumstances can turn around in an instant. So today, if you are going to make up a story about what will happen next in your life, make it a good story. Pre-pave the kind of future you want to live, no matter what the evidence to the contrary. The only future you want to visit in your mind's eye is a future where things are working out well for you. So change the story today and you just might be pleasantly surprised by what happens next.

4th December
Eccentricities

We all have our little quirks and foibles—personal eccentricities that to some may seem endearing but others may find irritating. They are part of our unique make-up that makes us the special beings that we are. Just because someone else thinks you shouldn't do it your way, that there is a better way or (what they usually mean) a more conservative way, doesn't make it wrong. If it doesn't cause any harm to you or anyone else, what does it matter? Today the JoyScope gives you permission to be all of who you are. Be the one who stands out from the crowd. Allow your uniqueness to shine. Those who tread a different path are the ones who are remembered most.

5th December
Body Love

The JoyScope invites you to love your body! There is a great deal of pressure for us to conform to an idealistic view of what we *should* look like. It is, therefore, sometimes less than easy to remember to appreciate all the good things our bodies do for us every day. Our body handles our breathing, regulates our heartbeat, digests food and supports all the other life-giving functions, without our conscious intervention. And even when we are unwell, our bodies are doing everything they can to self-heal. So today let go of any hang-ups and give thanks to your body for being just the way it is. Whatever the shape or form, your body is serving you pretty well. So flow some appreciation and love to your body today.

6th December
Imagination

The message from the JoyScope today is to feed your imagination. Everything that surrounds you now once started as a thought. The chair you sit on was once an idea in someone's mind. This book started as a creative thought. The greatest inventions and ideas grew out of pure imagination. Find ways to create more space in your mind for inspiration. Let go of any emotional and physical clutter that holds you back and focus on activities that nurture your creativity. You may just get to be pleasantly surprised at how quickly the ideas flood in. Where will your imagination take you today?

❦

7th December
Winning

Are you a winner in life? As soon as we mention winning, we conjure up thoughts that in some way our lives are a competition and that if we are to have winners in the world, we must also have losers. But that simply isn't true. Why? Because whatever the situation we face, we have a choice on our viewpoint. In fact, in every experience there is wanted and unwanted. Focus on the unwanted and you will feel like you are losing but focus on the wanted and it will seem as though you win. Therefore, the trick is to filter every experience for the hidden benefits. Our judgment is only ever a perception anyway so we can just choose to judge it differently. If there is a challenge or difficult situation unfolding in your life right now, be willing to seek the positives. What advantages could it bring with it? Change the story you are telling yourself and you may just find that you always win!

❦

8th December
True Vocations

The things that scare us most are often the things that we most need to do! If the thought of standing up to speak in front of a large audience turns your legs to jelly or you would love to start your own business but wonder how you would handle the uncertainty or you know you have a book inside you but worry what others would say, then beneath the fear may well hide your true vocation. It doesn't mean that you need to jump in with both feet, although this is certainly an option that has worked for those who have trodden the path before you. You can choose to take it step-by-step and still find yourself moving in the right direction. It doesn't have to be daunting or overwhelming. Simply start to think like a speaker, entrepreneur or author and notice what happens. Try answering the question *"what do you do?"* with your aspirational career rather than your current reality. How does it feel? Maybe, just maybe, it is something that you could allow yourself to grow into.

9th December
Embarrassing Moments

Today is confession time—what is the most embarrassing thing you have ever done? What makes your toes curl as you cringe in recalling what happened on that fateful day? Perhaps it even happened some time ago, but you can still feel the mortification even now. Want to know a secret? It was never really as shameful as you thought it was. You don't have to explain or justify what happened or why you did it. Give yourself a break. Remember that we give the meaning to events so you can just let it go or find a way to let yourself off the hook. How would you reassure a friend or loved one? Soothe yourself in the same way. If you look really closely, there may even be something to smile about. And if there is anyone who still holds it against you, remember the saying *"Those who mind don't matter, and those who matter don't mind"*!

10th December
Freedom of Choice

Life is based on the fundamental premise that we have freedom of choice. We get to make decisions and take actions that are right for us. We are as unique as our fingerprint so our choices will always be completely individual. However, we are sometimes inclined to forget this when the people around us are making their choices. It is a little too easy to want them to choose options that fit with what we want rather than what is right for them. Today give everyone permission to be their true authentic self around you. When we allow people to be all of who they are, we get to experience their full magnificence.

11th December
Love Letters

The writing of love letters is a lost art form. With emailing, texting and instant messaging, the need for a lengthy note has been replaced with the ability to say our feelings in a just a short phrase, often abbreviated into a few letters (some phones even have a list of statements that you can choose from rather than typing them out yourself!) It is amazing to be able to have instant communication available and for that, we can count the blessings of technology. But what if instead of making it a replacement for the love letter, we made it *in addition to*? There is something wonderful and intensely connecting about sending a message using traditional pen and paper. In some ways a hand-written note seems more permanent, more special and more significant. We take time to compose our thoughts in a different way when we are handwriting. We tend to communicate with more depth, sincerity and trust. So who deserves this special gift? Maybe you have a partner, a child, a family member or a close friend that would love to receive a token of your love? And, of course, perhaps the best love letter you can ever compose is the one addressed to you. Self-love is the greatest gift of all!

12th December
Control

OK, be honest. Are you a little bit of a control junkie? Do you secretly (or not so secretly) wish you had a way of making sure that every outcome goes your way? You are not alone. There aren't many people walking the planet who can say that they are comfortable with losing control. Where the problem lies is that being in control is just an illusion. You see you can never lose control of something that you never had in the first place. Life knows what we want and has our back but sometimes it simply doesn't work out the way you thought it was meant to. It may not be in your highest and best interests or it may not be the right time. It doesn't mean it isn't working. It is always happening perfectly. So if we don't have control of the outcome, what do we have control of? Simply the willingness to allow everything to unfold as it is meant to and feel the relief of ending the useless struggle for a power you can never own. As you let go, the truth will reveal itself, and that is the real win in life.

13th December
Ending Battles

Far too often we buy into the theory that we have to fight to get what we want. Effort and struggle are seen to be worthy approaches and we celebrate and honour people who have succeeded against the odds. It is uplifting to hear stories of people who have overcome adversity. But the last thing we really want is to engage in battles with people and our environment in an attempt to secure what we think we need. There is never a need to fight for what we want. There is more than enough to go around. So today let go of the struggle and competition. Wave the white flag and end the battles both within and without. Invite peace into your life.

14th December
Giving Gifts

For many people, this time of year is about buying and wrapping gifts ready for sharing on Christmas Day. But the greatest gift we can give to anyone is our pure and undivided attention. How many of us try to multi-task and find ourselves holding a conversation with a loved one, child or friend, whilst getting all the activities associated with the preparation for Christmas done at the same time? So today, whether you celebrate Christmas or not, give someone close to you the gift of your full focused attention, even if it is just for five minutes. Christmas will come and go. Our relationships can be everlasting when we invest wisely in them.

15th December
Special Effects

Have you ever watched a science fiction movie and been in awe of the special effects. Maybe, for a while, you were transported into a world where anything was possible. People travel back in time or into the future, have amazing gadgets and technology or find other life forms on planets far away. When the movie is really good, we may become so engrossed in the story that we temporarily forget what is real and what is fantasy. Without being aware, we may even lose sight of the awareness that the whole film is make believe! Life isn't really very different. We are always telling ourselves a story about what has happened or what will happen in the future. And, most of the time, that story is our very own fantasy based on our perceptions and our expectations. In truth, how much of it really happens? So today if you are going to make it up, make the fantasy a good one! Tell yourself a story of limitless possibilities that feeds your soul and enriches your life.

16th December
The Inside Job

For those who celebrate Christmas, the anticipation is now building with just nine more sleeps to go. But what if it doesn't feel exciting? For some people, life challenges get in the way (relationship difficulties, mounting debt or just the thought of spending a day with a dreaded relative!) and this makes it less than easy to be in a celebratory mood. But whether you love this time of year or whether you wish it would hurry up and be over, it is still possible to create whatever feelings you want to experience right now. You see, Christmas (and all other celebrations) is an inside job. Sure, it helps when life is moving along perfectly but even when it is not, you can make a conscious and deliberate decision to feel the way you want to feel without anything needing to change on the outside. So what would you choose from the menu today—peace, happiness, joy, tranquility, exhilaration, or ecstasy? The choice is yours!

17th December
Beyond Balance

One of the buzz concepts to emerge in the latter part of the 20th Century was the idea of work-life balance. It was widely recognised that when we pursued our career at the expense of the rest of our lives, our relationships, our health and our family lives suffered. Seeking balance was a useful concept for us to aim for. But is it balance that we really seek? When we think of balance, perhaps we imagine weighing options on a scale in an attempt to ensure they are equally distributed. We are trying to use an external process to handle our inner experiences. What we are usually seeking is an internal state of feeling centred and in control. Rather than trying to balance our lives, instead we can tune into the solid feelings of being grounded and let life flow from there. Paradoxically, when we do it that way, balance will tend to be the natural bi-product.

18th December
An Hour a Day!

Life is filled with so many exciting opportunities. It is possible to have a full and vibrant life. The real question then is how to have all of that whilst also experiencing joy and peace rather than feeling overwhelmed by how much there is to do? The trick is to simplify. That doesn't mean that you won't create big things, but if you keep the action part manageable you stay in your flow and can sustain the activity for the longer term. If you have a big project in mind—maybe you want to learn a new skill or develop a talent or write a book—just commit to doing an hour a day. It soon adds up and brings the big results!

19th December
Slowing Down to Speed Up

At this time of year, it can be a bit too easy to believe that there is too much to do and too little time. Everyone can start to get a tad crazy thinking that they will not be ready in time for the holidays. But have you ever noticed that as soon as you try to speed up, you seem to automatically slow down? You go to the shops but forget an essential item, you find yourself stuck in endless queues and somehow everything starts to go wrong or holds you up. In fact, the fastest way to get to where you want is usually to slow your pace down. When you take your time, you remember everything you need effortlessly and somehow the Universe seems to conspire with you to provide car park spaces, an absence of queues and great discounts on the things that you need. So today take your time and notice how you move easily into the flow.

20th December
Leadership

Being a leader isn't about having a big corporation, a position of power or millions in the bank. True leadership comes from your ability to inspire people to be the best they can be. That isn't about the work that you do—although that can certainly be one area to express your leadership. Some of the most powerful leadership that is transforming our culture is given by those people who are stepping up and becoming role models in families, in schools and as parents. If we do believe that the world hangs in a precarious balance, inspiring and leading others is going to be the fastest cure. We all have a leadership role to play. Today identify and focus on how you can make your contribution to the future of the planet.

21st December
Connection

When we are born, we are totally reliant on other people for our survival. As we age and particularly as we approach the end of our lives, we are also likely to find ourselves reliant on others to take care of all of our basic needs. The question is, are we really that different in between? Imagine if you were the only person on earth. Unless you are a would-be hermit, the prospect is probably not so appealing. We do rely on each other much more than we often acknowledge. When we embrace our connectedness, we are drawn more and more to create groups and communities that foster this interdependence. So the invitation from the JoyScope today is to reach out to others. Whether it is striking up a conversation with someone you don't know so well, reminding the people you care about why they matter, or even starting a new support group or network. Seize the opportunity to connect even more fully today.

22nd December
Setbacks

All set backs are temporary. Only quitting is ever permanent. There will always be times in our life when things don't appear to be going according to plan. Part of the joy of being human is the range of emotions that we experience. Only by knowing moments of despair or disappointment can we truly relish and bask in the joy of elation and bliss. We really do want the full spectrum of feelings—that is what gives us the juice of life. We simply need to remember that all things come to pass and when we are able to recognise that everything continues to change and evolve, we move over any blips much faster and more painlessly. Today if things don't seem to be working out quite as you want, just allow whatever will be to be, knowing that whatever the situation, better things are *all ways* on their way.

23rd December
Being Good Enough

There is a widespread myth that most of us have at some level and yet it is never usually talked about! The underlying belief that haunts us is that we don't believe we are good enough.

We may try and mask our feelings by acting confident or taking the one up position and putting others down, but deep down we still know that it is there. What it really comes down to is that we are holding a fundamental life position of not being OK. When you think about it, how bizarre is that? So the JoyScope today is here to remind you that you are good enough just the way you are. You were born that way and you will live that way until the close of play. Let go of the worry or concern that one day you might get *found out*. You were only ever being judged by your ego anyway.

24th December
Past Lives

Have you ever wondered who you might have been in a previous life? Maybe you believe in past lives or maybe you don't but either way it can be fun to play with the idea in your imagination. If you had been around the block before, who would you like to have been? Would you have been William Wallace who stood up so vehemently for his Scottish rights or Boudicca and her warrior attitude? Or perhaps Leonardo da Vinci and his artistic flair and creativity or Alexander Fleming who transformed the world of medicine with his discovery of antibiotics? Maybe Marilyn Munroe and her feminine charm or Martin Luther King and his ability to inspire? Often we are drawn to historical characters because of the qualities we think they embody and usually it is a tip off that we also possess those strengths inside if us. So, just for fun, write a list of who you think you could have been, identify the quality that they represent for you, and uncover the secrets of your subconscious identity.

25th December
Happy Christmas

On this day, the Universe sends to you...
12 breath-taking views
11 belly laughs
10 snuggles on the sofa
9 kisses under the mistletoe
8 leaps of faith
7 warm & fuzzy moments
6 pleasant surprises
5 reasons to believe
4 synchronicities
3 magic wishes
2 lifetime adventures
and a dose of pure appreciation of life!
Whether or not you celebrate Christmas, have a wonderful day!

26th December
Holidays

The holiday season is an interesting time of year. On the one hand you have the excitement and anticipation whilst on the other it may bring challenges and overwhelm. It may not come as much of a surprise to know that holidays don't always live up to the advertising hype of happy and loving families. You may have aggravating relatives or demanding children or be spending more time alone than perhaps you would want. So today the JoyScope wants to remind you of the importance of being happy. There is nothing more important than you feel good. Become aware of any drains on your positivity. Give yourself a day of rest from the doom and gloom of the news, abstain from engaging in conversations with complaining friends or family members and just turn a blind eye to any situations that leave you feeling less than inspired. Make today the day that you just choose to be happy—your gift to you!

27th December
Being Willing to Fall

Have you noticed how children aren't afraid to make mistakes? Whether it is a willingness to fall when taking their first steps or being prepared to ask questions that may seem daft or irrelevant. They have no fear. They are completely at ease with stepping out and speaking up. When does all of that change? When is it that we suddenly find ourselves less willing to ask a question for fear of looking stupid or naive? When do we stop taking risks in case we make a mistake? Being human is all about growing, and learning is part of that. Sometimes we may fall but that is only ever temporary, unless we decide to give up and not try again. Today you are invited to step into the unknown—do something you have never tried before or ask a question, no matter how dumb you think it may be. You never know, maybe you will discover something refreshingly new.

28th December
Breathing Through Overwhelm

There will always be times when life overwhelms us. Sometimes it's the big stuff like a redundancy or relationship break-up and sometimes it is just the accumulation of a number of smaller things that all seem to require our attention urgently. Yet when we try to speed up to handle them, it doesn't always work out so well. In fact, it can often seem like those issues come thicker and faster when we do. A much more aligning and gentle approach is to breathe our way through these situations. Pausing and inhaling deeply, centers us back in our bodies and reminds us that all of the other circumstances are temporary—*this too will pass!* Enjoy taking a deep breath of life today.

29th December
Your Worst Critic

Are you your own worst critic? Our perspective of ourselves is often totally inaccurate. Because we reside in our own bodies and minds, we are highly aware of every mistake or blunder we think we make and that can be a source of ongoing negative feedback. Most of the time, our expectations of ourselves are much higher than the standards we set for the people around us. So today the message is to *go easy on yourself.* We are all doing the best that we can and most of our slip-ups will go unnoticed by the rest of the world. And even if it is a more public mistake, you are only demonstrating your human-ness, which many will find endearing. Release the judgments on yourself and let the peace of mind flood in.

30th December
Feed Your Passion

How do you feed your passion? If we want an exciting and fun-filled life, we need to dedicate some of our time and energy to getting inspired. Too many of us get sucked into a life of mundaneness when there is so much to feel enthusiastic about: people to meet and connect with, places to visit and explore, adventures and journeys to have. When you consider the multitude of possibilities, how do we ever find time to get bored? Take the opportunity to create a rich banquet of treats for you to enjoy. What would you put on the menu? Feed your passion and get ridiculously inspired about your life today.

31st December
Surrendering to Divinity

Do you sense your connection to the Divine? When we disconnect from the source energy of all that is, our lives become an uphill struggle. We slip into patterns of fighting and pushing for what we want, rather than allowing and accepting. Bizarrely, the more that we surrender to what is, the more we invite the very objects and experiences that we desire to find us. Surrender is not the same as giving up. Surrender is the willingness to turn challenges and situations to a higher power, trusting that everything will unfold perfectly. Even when things don't appear to be going to plan, it is the willingness to stay trusting and have faith that it will work out. So today the JoyScope would like you to scan your life and find the places where you are hanging on to old battles or struggles. When you discover these energy drains, just gently let go. Say, "*I release this experience. Thank you. I love you*", and move on. Let go. Let it be. Let love in!

Further information:

For information on products, events, workshops and coaching with Tiffany Kay, please visit the website tiffanykay.com